BRONSKI

SPECIAL INVESTIGATOR

U. S. ARMY

L. Cortney Rick-Burge

BRONSKI
SPECIAL INVESTIGATOR
U.S.ARMY

A LUCKY BEAR BOOK

Published by LUCKY BEAR ENTERPRISES, INC.
P.O.Box 2506, Sparks, Nevada 89432-2506

PUBLISHER"S NOTE: This book is a work of fiction. Names, characters, places, and incidents either are the product of the author's imagination or are used fictitiously, and any resemblance to actual persons, living or dead, events, or locals are coincidental.

.

Second Printing, March 1998

ISBN: 0-9653398-0-7

LCCN: 96-77518

DEDICATION:

I WISH TO DEDICATE THIS BOOK

TO
LT. COL. JESSE NAPIER, CAP

AND
MAJOR JAMES NICHOLSON, CAP

FOR THEIR HELP AND ENCOURAGEMT.

TO
ALL MY FRIENDS WHO ENCOURAGED
ME TO HAVE THIS BOOK PUBLISHED.

TO
CYNTHIA RYAN
WHO GAVE ME THE BENEFIT OF HER
WONDERFUL TALENTS AND EXPERIENCE
BY DESIGNING THE COVER.

TO
CONNIE LAPIERRE GLASHAN, 1ST LT CAP
FOR HER HELP AND ENCOURAGEMENT

AND

LAST BUT NOT LEAST,
TO
SAM LYNCH
FOR HIS OPTIMISM ABOUT
THE SUCCESS OF THIS BOOK.

ABOUT THE AUTHOR

Born Lyle Cortney Burge, March 13, 1916, at Centralia, Illinois. He was raised and educated in Chicago. After completing high school in 1934, he and a buddy "bummed" their way out to California, stopping on the way to work on the Boulder Dam for a short time. On the way he picked up the name "Ricky". Over the years it has been cut short to "Rick". So many people know him by that name that he made it legal by changing his birth certificate to read Lyle Cortney Rick-Burge. Thus the "Nom de Plum", L. Cortney Rick-Burge. He was married in 1935. He became the first welding apprentice in the U.S.Steel Corporation in 1936. Continuing his education with evening and correspondence courses he received a degree in engineering. He learned to fly in 1940 by helping the mechanic at a small airfield in his spare time, doing his welding for him. Rick later flew with the Army Air Corps. He is a commercial, instrument rated, certified flight instructor. In his over fifty years of flying, he has flown more than forty five different types of aircraft and logged almost 12,000 hours. He has been flying for the Civil Air Patrol for over twenty four years as a mission and check pilot. He has worked as a draftsman, engineer, and ironworker. Moving to Nevada in 1954, he started a steel fabricating business doing ornamental iron and special fabrication. He retired in 1985, but still manages to keep busy.

Rick began his writing when he first met one of his grandsons, then five years old, who asked, "What did you do before I met you, Grandpa?" To which he relied, "Someday I'll write my autobiography and I'll tell you all about myself." The grandson is now the father of two and Rick has yet to finish his autobiography, though he works on it occasionally.

Rick has one son still living, who is also a pilot, and three talented daughters. He has fourteen grandchildren and seventeen great grandchildren, with one more on the way. He has a step-daughter and a step-son, five step-grandchildren and one step-great granddaughter. He is single and has been living in Reno, Nevada for the past forty two years.

BRONSKI
SPECIAL INVESTIGATOR
U. S. ARMY

CONTENTS

Part One
"Operation Boom"

Part Two
"Operation Sharp Shooter"

Part Three
"Operation Find A Gun"

Part Four
"Operation Foiled Mission"

PART ONE

"Operation Boom"

"Toro"

"OPERATION BOOM"

Fort Rycker, Alabama - 13 March

Pvt. Terry Smith pulled up to Gen. Henry Trackwell's house at 0700 sharp, jumped out of the car, and trotted up to the door. Before he could knock, the door opened and Martha Trackwell stood framed in the doorway, dressed in a thin slinky negligee. She greeted him in her soft, husky, sexy voice. "Good morning, Terry."

He gulped. "Good morning, Mrs. Trackwell, is the General ready?"

"Not quite, Terry, come in and have a cup of coffee while you wait."

Private Smith removed his cover and eased past her. She led him to the breakfast nook and indicated a chair. He couldn't take his eyes off of her as she poured the coffee.

She smiled to herself.

"When you get the General settled, would you come back here, Terry, I have something I would like you to help me with."

Private Smith blushed, he knew what she had in mind. She'd asked his help before. Martha was twenty years younger than the General.

"Sure, Mrs. Trackwell, I could be back about 0900."

Several minutes later the General walked in. "I'm ready when you are, Terry. Finish your coffee."

"Right away, Sir." He gulped down his coffee.

Private Smith held the door for the General then ran around to the driver's side. Two MP's drove by and waved. Terry returned their greeting. He took one last look at Martha, got in the car, started the engine, and began to pull away. At that moment the car disintegrated in a ball of flame.

The force of the explosion drove Martha back into the house against a wall. Windows were shattered and shards of glass flew everywhere.

Within minutes the area was swarming with fire fighting apparatus and military police. Pieces of the car were

1

scattered over a wide area and only pieces of the two men could be found. The whole section of the block was roped off. Martha Trackwell was rushed to the base hospital.

Gen. George Harris held an emergency meeting in his office.

"I want to know what happened out there and I want to know fast." He was talking to his Chief of Staff, Col. James Leer. To his aide, Lt. Richard Fitch, he said, "Get the OSI (Office of Special Investigatoins) on the phone and tell them to get every bomb expert they have on this case and get them down here in a hurry. God damn it, we can't have someone blowing up our generals. Hell, who knows who might be next?"

Lt. Fitch returned a few minutes later. "Sir, Capt. Bronski is on his way here from Fort Clark, he's the best explosive expert they have. He should be here this afternoon. I'll have a car ready to pick him up at the air strip.

"Very good, Fitch, get hold of Col. Hart and have him pick him up. I'd like him to work with Bronski. I want some action on this quick."

"With Capt. Bronski on the case, Sir, I'm sure you'll get it."

"CHAPTER TWO"

Capt. Joe Bronski, thirty years old, five feet ten, medium but powerful build, dark wavey hair, and deep hazel eyes that made men step back when he got that look in them.

Bronski was raised in Brooklyn, finished high school, worked his way through college for a degree in chemical engineering, then went on to get a degree in law.

A gang war bomb had accidently killed his father, mother, and younger sister when he was fifteen so he made a diligent study of explosives. By the time he was out of college he could examine an explosion and tell from the fragments what kind of explosive was used-whether foreign or domestic-how it was detonated, and give enough information to the investigators to aid in the apprehension of the culprits.

Bronski joined the Army in 1942, and immediately after completing basic training was sent to officers' training school. Upon graduating he was assigned to the Ordnance Divison for the study and design of explosives. When the war ended he transfered to the IG Division. Joe was an expert investigator. He uncovered minute clues that other investigators completely overlooked. He solved numerous cases for the Army that had been considered unsolvable.

In the hospital, Martha Trackwell was diagnosed as having suffered a concussion, a broken arm, four broken ribs, and a fractured leg. She had been treated, and casts were applied while she was still unconcious,

Gen. Trackwell's aide, Lt. Bart Nichols, and his wife, Nancy, were at her side when she regained conciousness.

"What happened? Where am I?"

"Lie still, Mrs. Trackwell, there's been an explosion and you were hurt. You're in the hospital."

"Where's Henry?" her eyes opening wide.

"I'm sorry, Mrs. Trackwell, but I'm afraid Henry was killed in the explosion, both he and Pvt. Smith, his driver."

3

"Oh, my God!" she cried, bursting into uncontrollable sobbing. Nancy tried to comfort her and after awhile she regained some of her composure. "I remember now, Henry and Terry had gotten into the car and were pulling away then suddenly there was an explosion and I was driven back into the house. That's all I remember until now. Oh, how horrible, poor Henry and Terry."

"The investigators will probably want to talk to you so try to remember everything you can. Nancy will stay with you. I have to get back to the office and talk to them, but I'll be back later. Nancy will get you anything you need."

"Thank you, Bart, I'll try to remember."

When he was gone she took hold of Nancy's hand. "Oh, Nancy, how terrible. I hope they didn't suffer. I wonder what could have caused such an awful thing?"

"I don't know, Mrs. Trackwell, but I'm sure they'll find out. Try to get some rest now, I'll be right here with you."

Two jeeps with MP's, a car, Pvt. Lind, the driver, and Col. Bret Hart from Operations, were at the air strip when the Cessna 310 touched down lightly on the runway and followed the jeep with the "Follow Me" sign on the back to the parking ramp. Joe Bronski jumped down off of the wing while the two ground crewmen set wheel chocks, then proceeded to tie the plane down.

Bronski unlocked the baggage compartment and removed his bag then turned to meet Col. Hart.

"Capt. Bronski, Bret Hart. I've been assigned to assist you in whatever way I can."

"Good to meet you, Colonel, can you tell me a little about what happened?"

They walked to the car where Pvt. Lind was holding the door open for them.

Bronski had no sooner sat down when he jumped up, grabbing both Hart and Lind, rushing them several feet from the car, and throwing them to the ground. At almost the same moment the car exploded. They were showered with pieces of hot metal, one jeep was turned on its side

4

dumping the MP's, and the two crewmen were knocked off their feet. The plane was skewed sideways, straining at the tiedown ropes. "What the hell happened?" exclaimed Hart.

"I smelled explosives the minute I got in the car. On the presumption It was going to blow, I dragged you two away with me. Is anyone hurt?"

Pvt. Lind was holding his hand. "Let me see that!" said Bronski. A piece of hot metal had landed on his hand and burned it rather severely.

"Who the hell was that meant for, you or me?" asked Hart.

"Since I'm here to investigate the explosion this morning, it was probably meant for me, but until we find out more, let's assume it was meant for both of us. In the meantime, CYA (cover your ass), and be careful."

In minutes fire apparatus and an ambulance were there. Col. Hart flagged the ambulance. "I don't think anyone else is hurt so take Pvt. Lind to the hospital and see that his hand is taken care of. Looks like he got a pretty bad burn."

A car arrived just then with Gen. Harris and Col. Leer. The General got out of the car without waiting for the driver to open the door.

"Is anyone hurt?" he asked, looking at Hart and Bronski.

"Yes, my driver got a bad burn on his hand, Sir, but I think the rest of us are all right, thanks to the Captain here. This is Capt. Bronski, Sir. Capt. Bronski, Gen. Harris, the Fort Commander."

Bronski saluted and they shook hands.

"Glad to see you here, Captain, now you two have two explosions to work on."

"I think I can tell you right now that this one was the same as the one this morning and set off remotely by someone nearby. I don't suppose there's a chance in hell of finding out who was in this area in the past hour. I don't know which one of us they were after but it was someone that knew when I would arrive."

"I've already had the Fort sealed off, no one can get in or out, not even me. I've ordered our best men to guard the perimeter and to shoot anyone who tries to disobey them."

"Fine, have this area sealed off for a hundred yards in diameter and don't let anyone touch anything. I want to go over and inspect this morning's site. I hope it has been secured."

"It has, even the houses in the immediate area have been vacated and the occupants put up in the BOQ," said the General.

"Good, I'll want to question them. Were any of them hurt?"

"Mrs. Trackwell sustained some injuries when the blast drove her back in the house. She's at the base hospital."

"I'll want to talk to her. Is she able to have visitors and talk?"

"I think so, but you can check with the doctor."

"Would you know if the local police have any dogs for sniffing bombs?"

"I'll have Fitch check on it right away."

"Can we walk to the first blast site? I'm a little gun shy of your autos. I'd suggest that none of them be used until they're gone over with a fine tooth comb."

They walked to where Gen. Trackwell's car had blown up. The area had been taped off for the entire block. Bronski ducked under the tape and indicated to Col. Hart to accompany him. The others started to follow.

"Hold it, I don't want anyone else in here until we're finished. I'm sorry, but one of you might pick up a valuable piece of evidence on your shoe without knowing it or disturb something you don't see. I'll show you everything we find later and we can go all over them."

Bronski and Hart walked slowly back and forth from one edge of the area to the other, occasionally stopping to pick up small pieces of debris and place them in plastic bags which Bronski produced. They searched until dark and then returned to where Gen. Harris and the others were waiting

6

"Do you think you found anything of value while you were searching?" asked the General, anxiously.

"Yes, Sir, I think we have. I can't tell you who or why, but I can tell you what and how. Let's go to your office, Sir, and I'll lay it all out for you. I think you'll find it interesting."

"I'll take care of that stuff for your, Captain," offered Col. Leer.

"NO, I'll hang on to it until we've gone over it, then you can have it," said Bronski, looking at him suspiciously.

"CHAPTER THREE"

Gen. Harris summoned Gen. Lewis, Gen. Willis, Gen. Hoyt, and Col. Hansen, Chief of Security, to meet in the board room . He introduced Capt. Bronski.

Bronski opened the plastic bags that he and Col. Hart had collected evidence in and spread the contents out on the table.

As he laid out each piece of evidence he explained its significance. "The explosive was German made, KXG 76. The detonator, a D7RE10, domestic made, was activated by remote, most likely an RELR12, also domestic made. This can activate the detonator within a range of about one mile. There are only three manufacturers of these domestic items and I have their names so it shouldn't be hard to trace the buyers. as soon as we check the blast at the air strip, I'll bet my boots that we'll find the same evidence. From the force, I figured a one pound charge was used."

Searching the area at the air strip produced the identical evidence.

Bronski turned to Hart. "Someone in this camp is a murderer. What we need to find out is the motive. I want to talk to Mrs. Trackwell, and the other residents on the street, the two ground crewmen at the air strip, your driver, and the MP's that were there."

Martha was able to see visitors and the doctor said he could question her, but not to make it too long. The next morning he went with Col. Hart to see her."

"Good morning, Mrs. Trackwell, I'm Capt. Bronski and I guess you know Col. Hart. I'm from the OSI office and I would like to ask you some questions if you feel up to it. But first let me offer my condolences for the loss of your husband and your injuries."

"How do you do, Captain, and thank you for your concern. What can I tell you?"

"I'd like you to tell me everything you can remember about yesterday morning, who you saw, and what you saw.

Tell me everything you can remember, even if you don't feel it's important."

Martha related the events of the morning from the time she got up until the blast.

"Very good, Mrs. Trackwell, but are you sure you haven't forgotten anything or left anything out?"

She thought for several minutes. "I don't think so. Wait, yes, there was something else, two MP's went by in a jeep just a moment before Henry and Terry got in the car. They go by every morning at the same time, that's why I didn't think of it."

"Did they do anything unusual, like slow up and take an extra look at the General and Pvt. Smith?"

"Well, they waved as they went by and Terry waved back."

Bronski had written all this down in shorthand as they talked. Thank you, Mrs. Trackwell, you've been very helpful. Again, my sympathies, and I hope you recover soon "

"Thank you, Captain, and I hope you're successful in your investigation."

Bronski questioned all the residents from the street near the Trackwell house, but none could offer anything worthwhile.

At the air strip he questioned the crewmen that had been there when the car exploded.

They couldn't offer much except one of them remembered that one of the jeeps with the MP's drove away just before the explosion.

Bronski and Hart ran down the two MP's that the crewman had recognized, Sgt. Carl Krase, and Corp. James Davis.

"Why did you start to drive off before the other jeep?" he asked the sergeant.

"I saw you get in the car and we were going to lead off to escort you to the General's headquarters.

"Do you make the rounds in the residential areas?"

"Sometimes."

"How about yesterday morning?"

"Yes, we passed just before the car blew up. Scared the hell out of us."

Bronski made a note of this and to himself he asked, why they didn't stop to investigate. He'd go into that later.

"I hope you can read that shorthand stuff," laughed Hart

Bronski smiled. "It's the only way I can get all the information down."

CHAPTER FOUR

Col. Hart suggested they stop at the "O Club" for lunch.

"Who would hate Gen. Trackwell enough to want to kill him?" asked Bronski..

"I don't know," answered Hart, "he was a good general and well liked. I just can't think of a reason why anyone would hate him."

"Someone had a reason and then tried to prevent me from investigating. Just between you and me, it's someone on the base that we would hardly suspect. How many generals do you have?"

"Four, Maj. General Harris, Lt. Gen. Willis, B/Gen. Lewis, and B/Gen. Hoyt. Col. Leer could be promoted to fill Gen. Trackwell's slot."

"I think they should have twentyfour hour security and their cars checked over thoroughly before they use them."

"I'll see that it's taken care of right away." He signaled for a waiter. "Would you bring me a phone, please?" The waiter brought him a cordless phone. "I'll call Col. Hansen, head of Base Security. You met him at the meeting yesterday."

He dialed a number. "Hello, Ed, Bret Hart here. I'm with Capt. Bronski from OSI. He wants twentyfour hour protection for all our generals, and their cars gone over before they use them. What? Fine, Ed, take care of it right away. I'll check with you later."

"Good," said Bronski, "I want a security check run on all the MP's."

"We already have a security check on them."

"Yes, but I want an update. I'll have my office take care of it."

A corporal came up to their table. "Pardon me, Sir, are you Capt. Bronski?"

"Yes, Corporal, I am."

"Gen. Harris wants to see you and Col. Hart in his office as soon as you finish your lunch, Sir."

11

"Thank you, Corporal."

Lt. Fitch announced their arrival at the office.

"Come in, Gentlemen," said the General,and motioned them to a couple of chairs. "First of all, Lt. Fitch checked with the local police. They don't have any dogs, but they have bomb expert."

"We don't need another bomb expert, and I doubt very much if he would know anything about what we're dealing with. If I can use your phone, I think I can have a couple of dogs here by morning," said Bronski.

The General indicated the phone. "Help yourself."

"Do you have a scrambler?" Bronski asked.

"Yes, push the button on the side of the phone."

Bronski picked up the phone and dialed his office number.

"Good afternoon, OSI."

"Hello, Mona, Joe here. Is Charley handy?"

"Yes, he is, Joe, I'll ring him for you. He just went into his office. How's it going?"

"Not good, but not bad, so far."

"Here's Charley. Good luck, Joe, and be careful."

"Hi, Joe, what can I do for you?"

"I need a couple of sniffers quick," said Bronski.

"No problem, Joe, I'll fly them down myself as soon as I can get them to the airport. I'll be in the King Air."

"Great, Charley, I want to talk to you anyhow. We'll meet you at the air strip. What time do you figure you'll be here?"

"I should be there about 2000 hours."

"Good, and thanks."

"Anything I can bring you?"

"Yeah, Mona, if she's free," he said, smiling.

"See you soon," Charley said, laughing. They broke the connection.

The General smiled. "Sounds like you know him quite well, Captain."

"We drop the formalities except when we're working among others. It isn't the rank we hold, it's how well we do our job."

"May I ask who Mona is?"

"The prettiest most efficient girl I've ever had the privilege to know. She's our all-around girl in the office, receptionist, switchboard operator, secretary, and analyst. She works for all of us. I should, say, with because at times, we feel we're working for her. A real gem. If you want to know something about somebody, give her an hour and she'll tell you his life history."

"I wish I were that lucky, I'm stuck with Fitch," he laughed, "not pretty, but efficient as hell, and stiff necked. I'm glad he's not my boss. I assigned Col. Hart to you because he's a good man, doesn't let any moss grow under his feet."

"Thank you, Sir, we seem to get along and work well together."

"Very well, Gentlemen, keep me informed, and let me know if there's anything I can do."

Bronski and Hart rose and were dismissed.

Outside, Hart asked, "What do you think of the Old Man?"

"He'll do, I like his eyes, they're straight-forward. He's worried about these explosions, I can see it in his eyes even though he tries to hide it," said Bronski

"I didn't realize you were so observant, Captain."

"Shall we drop the rank when we're working alone? It will make it easier to work together. I'm Joe."

"Suits me fine. I'm Bret."

At 2000 hours, the big King Air made it's approach to the air strip. After it touched down and rolled out, the jeep with the "Follow Me" sign led it to the parking ramp.

As soon as the props stopped turning, Bronski and Hart approached the left side. The door swung open and two German Shephards trotted down the stairs that the ground crewmen pulled out, followed by their handlers. Charley Blake followed them.

13

A word and the dogs sat by the side of their handlers.

Bronski extended his hand. "Hi, Charley, meet Col. Bret Hart. Bret, Maj. Charley Blake."

"Major, my pleasure."

"And mine, Colonel. Can we go some place and talk?"

"Let's get back in the plane," said Bronski, "I'll have the handlers go over the car while we're talking."

"Let me get the dogs' rations out of the plane first, Sir, if you don't mind," said one of the sergeants.

"No, go ahead." They unloaded two crates. Bronski, Hart, and Blake got in the plane.

When they were seated Charley asked, "what can I do for you, Joe?"

Bronski told him about the two explosions and what they had found.

"I'd like you to run down all the sources of KXG 76 plastic, D7RE10 detonators, and RELR12 remote units. See if you can find out who has purchased any of these in the past year. They may have been purchased recently but I think whoever the culprits are have been planning this for a long time."

"They may have been purchased recently but that would make them too easy to trace. Check all the black market dealers and terrorist orgs you can find. Bang a few heads or break a few arms if you have to, but we need that information fast. I'm sure Trackwell wasn't the only target and they haven't made the last try on Bret and me."

Charley had been taking all this down in shorthand. Bret smiled and shook his head. "I'll have to learn that."

"Got it, Joe. As soon as I'm airborne, I'll get on the phone and get the ball rolling. Meantime, you two, CYA." They shook hands, then Bronski and Hart exited the plane.

Blake waved from the cockpit as he started the engines and taxied out. As soon as he was in the air, Joe and Bret turned to their car. Pvt. Lind was standing with the handlers and their two dogs by the hood.

"What's up, Sergeant?" asked Bronski.

"I think Toro has found something under the hood, Sir."

"OK, move away while I open it. " He tripped the hood latch then went around the front to lift it.

"Bring the dog over here and see how he acts.

Toro put his paws on the fender and sniffed the firewall. Bronski looked it over but saw nothing but a smudge. He rubbed his finger over it and sniffed. He held it for the dog to smell. He sniffed and whined.

"Someone had some plastic explosive in here then removed it. Let's see who has been near this car in the past several hours." Bronski turned to Pvt. Lind. "Get on your radio and call for another car for the handlers and their dogs." To the two sergeants he said, "I'm Capt. Bronski, and this is Col. Hart. You'll work strickly for us, and you'll take orders only from us, not even the General."

"Yes, Sir. I'm Sgt. Peel and this is Sgt. Ward. These are the best two dogs in the service. If there's explosives around, they'll find it. Their names are Toro and Raz."

"Good, I hope they find it in time. I have a feeling they're going to be busy. Here comes your car, check it over good before you get in it."

The car pulled up and the two dogs checked it over. "It's clean, Sir," said Ward. "Wait until we load their rations and we'll be ready. Is there someplace we can store it where it will be secure?"

"I'm sure we can find a place, and I know what you mean.," said Bronski. "We'll go over to the motor pool and check out the vehicles. Have you or the dogs had dinner yet? Hell, what am I talking about, how could you, you were on the plane. We'll get something to eat and then check the motor pool. Head over to the "O Club", Lind. Follow us, fellows."

The "O Club" manager started to stop them when they entered with the dogs. Hart held up his hand. "It's all right, Fredrick, these are special dogs from the OSI and their handlers. They can't be left alone and unguarded. They're

15

working with us on these bombings, so find us a table in the corner, please."

The two sergeants smiled as they walked through the dining room with Toro and Raz. The dogs walked along beside them, paying no attention to anyone. When they were seated the dogs sat beside them with their backs to the table.

"Do you ever feed them at the table?" asked Hart.

"No, Sir, they wouldn't take it if we did. I'll show you in a minute," said Sgt. Peel.

"How do you like your steaks?" asked Bronski.

They both smiled. "Medium rare for me, Sir," said Peel. "Same for me, Sir," replied Ward.

When the steaks arrived, Sgt. Peel cut off a small piece.

"Let me show you what I mean, Sir," he offered the steak to Toro. The dog sat like a statue and ignored the morsel.

"He loves steak, too, Sir. Do you see how well they're trained? He wouldn't take anything from anyone but me if he was starving. Eliminates the danger of someone trying to poison them."

"I'm impressed," smiled Hart, "I wish we could train our men as well. Present company accepted."

"Accepted, Sir," smiled Peel.

They had a lot of strange looks from the officers that were eating in the dining room, but nothing was said.

They entered the motor pool and went through all of the vehicles, but found them clean.

"All right for now," said Bronski, "we'll get you a room at the BOQ so you'll be close, and pick you up about 0500. We'll come back here after breakfast and go over each vehicle before anyone can check it out. I'll leave orders that none of them are to be released until we check them."

"CHAPTER FIVE"

At 0500 the two sergeants and their dogs were ready to go when Bronski and Hart met them at the front door.

"Good morning, men," Bronski greeted them.

"Good morning, Sirs."

"Let's go get some breakfast. Have the dogs been fed?"

"Yes, Sir, we feed them first thing in the morning and a snack at night."

"Good, then that leaves just us, let's go."

As soon as they finished breakfast they headed for the motor pool. Each vehicle was checked over by the dogs before it was released to the driver.

"I want one of you to stay here and check each vehicle before it is started and moved out. The drivers have orders not to leave their vehicles at anytime unless we have someone to relieve them. If anyone gives you trouble, draw your piece and place them under arrest, then send for one of us. That goes for everyone, from the General on down. The other one will come with us and we'll check every vehicle on the base, moving or parked," said Bronski.

"I'll stay here, Sir," volunteered Ward.

"Fine, you have your orders, keep sharp."

"Yes, Sir," he replied, smiling.

"Major Blake briefed us on the way here, how you work ,and the way you like things done, so we'll do a good job for you, Sir, " explained Ward.

Bronski smiled. "Saves me a lot of talking, doesn't it?"

Both Peel and Ward grinned. "Yes, Sir."

Bronski, Hart, and Sgt. Peel with Toro, spent the day checking and rechecking all the vehicles on the base. Everything was quiet for the moment.

"CHAPTER SIX"

At 0500 the phone in Bronski's room came to life. He just woke up when ut started ringing.

"Bronski, here," he answered.

"Captain, you had better get down here to my office quick, this is Col. Hansen at Security."

"All right, Colonel, I'll get Col. Hart and be right down." He broke the connection and dialed Hart's room. "Hansen just called, all excited. "I'll get the sergeants and meet you down in front."

A car was waiting for them when they stepped out the door.

"Where the hell did get this car?" demanded Bronski.

The MP, Sgt. Clancy, who was holding the door, answered, "From the motor pool. Col. Hansen sent me to pick it up for you, Sir."

"Damn it, I gave orders no vehicles were to be taken out until they were checked over by the dogs. Peel, Ward, have the dogs check it out." Toro and Raz went over the car but found nothing.

"All right, let's go."

Col. Hansen met them as they pulled up. "Come with me," he said, and started around the building. When they rounded the corner they spotted a body.

"Found him this morning, just by accident," said Hansen.

Bronski and Hart approached the dead man. "This is one of the MP's we questioned yesterday, Corp. Davis."

Bronski turned the body over and patted his pockets. From one he removed an RELR12 remote unit.

"Looks like you've found at least one of your blasters. But who killed him and why?" asked Hansen.

"Let's go into your office, Colonel, I need to use your phone. Does it have a scrambler?" asked Bronski.

"Yes, it does, come on in."

Bronski flipped on the scrambler and dialed his office number.

"Good morning, OSI."

"Hi, Mona, Joe, is Charley around?"

"Hello, Joe, how're things going? I'll ring Charley for you."

"Good and bad, Mona, but I need some information from Charley to make it better."

"I'm praying for you, Joe. Here's Charley."

"Hi, Joe, what's up?"

"Did you run a check on those two names I gave you?"

"Got them right here, what do you need?"

"Tell me what you have on Corp. James Davis."

"I'll read you the report on him." He read the report. "Do you have something on this fellow?"

"No, he's been murdered and I found a remote unit, RELR12 in his pocket. Smells like a plant. Somebody's trying to throw me off the track. Thanks, Charley, I'll keep in touch."

He hung up the phone and turned to Hart. "Charley checked this kid out real good. He's never been around explosives in his life. Someone planted that remote on him to make us think he was guilty them murdered him to cover it up. Our killer is someone in this camp that we don't suspect and has a desperate reason. Ward, you take Raz and get back to the motor pool. See if any one has checked out a vehicle. If they have give me a call and we'll go check it out. If Pvt. Lind is there, send him back to pick us up."

Ward called in about fifteen minutes. "Three cars have gone out, Sir, Gen. Wills', Gen. Hoyt 's, and Col. Leer's. They haven't been gone long. Pvt. Lind is on his way to pick you up."

"Thanks, Sergeant, stay alert." He turned to Hart and Peel then told them what Ward had said. "Let's go check out Gen. Willis' car first. Come on, let's go."

As they turned the corner onto the street where Willis' car was they saw the General and his driver get in and start to pull away. A moment later an explosion racked the air and the car was enveloped in a ball of flames. Pvt. Lind slammed on the brakes, but their car was showered with debris.

"Oh, my God!" exclaimed Hart, "They didn't have a chance."

"Did any of you see anything?" asked Bronski.

"Yes, Sir, that jeep just got away just in time," said Lind.

"What Jeep?" demanded Bronski.

"I'm sure I saw one going just ahead of the General's car, looked like MP's."

"Quick, back out and see if you can catch that jeep!" hollered Bronski.

"What's on your mind?" asked Hart as they sped after the jeep.

"I have a hunch whoever is setting off those explosions is in a vehicle. Didn't a jeep pass Trackwell's car? And weren't there two jeeps at the airstrip? And now one here," asked Bronski. "Who ever it is knows when the cars leave the motor pool and who's car it is."

They quickly covered the area, but couldn't locate the jeep.

"Go back to Security and we'll find out which MP's are out in jeeps and how many are usually on patrol in the morning," said Bronski.

They met Col. Hansen heading for the explosion site and stopped.

"What the hell happened this time?" he asked.

"Gen. Willis just got it. Have your men tape off the area and see if anyone is injured," said Bronski.

At the Security office they checked the duty roster for the names of the MP's on patrol. Sgt. Larry Miller, Corp. Mike O'Brien, Sgt. Carl Krase, Corp. Allen King, Sgt. William Porter, and Corp. Donald Hill were on

20

duty. Bronski picked up the phone, turned on the scrambler, and dialed his office. He gave the names to Blake and got the report on Sgt. Krase.

"Looks like we can scratch Krase off our list of suspects, from this report I doubt if he's ever fired a firecracker. We'll have to wait and see what Charley comes up with on these others. Let's get back to the bomb scene, I want to see if our bomber is using the same material on all of these jobs."

Bronski and Hart searched through the wreckage and found that the same detonators and explosive were used as on the other explosions.

"Looks like our boy has a good supply of material. Maybe we should look for his cache.," said Bronski. "Whoever he is, he knows about explosives. I think we should check the personnel files and see what we can come up with. First let's go back to the motor pool and see if we can find out who was in there early this morning or during the night."

"There are a lot of men on this base, it will take a long time to sort through all the files," replied Hart.

"Did I say this was going to be easy? We can let Peel take Toro in the car and check the rest of the vehicles."

When they reached the motor pool, Ward met them at the door. "Jeez, Sir, I've been trying to locate you, we've got another one."

Ward led them to a staff car with the trunk lid open. A body was stuffed inside.

"Have you found out who he is?" asked Bronski.

"Yes, Sir, he's one of the motor pool men that was on duty last night, Corp. Tom Kennedy. Raz was sniffing around and stopped here so I opened the trunk and there he was. I also found this." It was a D7RE10 detonator. "I knew it was a detonator so I disarmed it."

"Where was it?" asked Bronski.

"It was stuck in this stuff. I thought it was plastic but Raz didn't react to it. I knew this was a detonator so rather than take a chance, I pulled it out."

Bronski took the plastic mass out and smelled it. "No

wonder he couldn't react to it, it's been sprayed with Clorox. Can you train him to detect that?"

"Yes, Sir, with about two hours of training and they'll be able to pick up that smell out of a garbage dump," replied Ward.

"Good, our boy is getting cute. You start training the dogs, but in the meantime we'll have to physically inspect all the vehicles. I'll get some information from my office that might help you." He checked the corpse. "This guy is also very adept with a knife, all the victims have been killed with one stab in a vital spot."

Gen. Harris blew a fuse when he heard about the two murders and Gen. Willis getting killed. He sent for Bronski and Hart.

"What the damn hell is happening, Captain? Why are my generals getting blown up and personnel getting murdered?"

"I wish I had the answer, Sir, but I'm working on a theory. Who is in line for these general slots?" asked Bronski.

"Well, let's see, Col. Leer, Col. Burton, Col. Fertig, Col. Evans, and Col. Hart."

"We can scratch Col. Hart, he's been my shadow since I've been here. What I'm thinking is someone is knocking off generals to make room for a promotion. The two corporals may have been killed because they found out too much or witnessed something," said Bronski.

The General shook his head as if in disbelief. "I was going to say that you're being ridiculous, but the more I think about it the more I think there's meat in your theory. I find it hard to point a finger at any of those men. Their records are spotless."

"I'll have my office check all of them. In the meantime, I have a plan I'd like to lay out for you and Col. Hart. All of these men have aides-de-camp, right?"

"Yes, go on," queried the General.

"Suppose I bring in some operatives to replace these aides. You could promote them and move them into another section. I'm sure they're all good men and promotions wouldn't cast any suspicions. There must be someplace I could bring these men in and place them for a few days without any questions," said Bronski. "Hart, you should be able to arrange that. The ones I have in mind will do an excellent job and quickly gain the confidence of the colonels."

"By God, if you ever get tired of working for the OSI, Bronski, I'll have a top notch position for you. How about you two being my guests for dinner tonight?"

"There will be three of us, General. Major Blake will be with us. I'm sure you will be impressed with him, Sir, he knows which fork to use."

"That would be your friend and fellow conspirator, Charley?"

"Yes, Sir."

"Good, I'll expect you at 1800 hours, casual dress. You'll love my wife Emily, she loves having younger men around."

Bronski got on the General's phone and called his office, using the scrambler.

"Hi, Mona, Joe here, how are you, love?"

"Joe, I'm fine. How are you, sweet? What can I do for you?"

"Rustle up Charley for me, but first can you locate Jim Gutterman, Paul Bender, Bary Walls, and Jerry Brennan? When you do, tell them to dig out their shavetail uniforms and be prepared to fly down with Charley."

"No sooner said than done, all four are in the conference room having coffee. Charley will be with you in a minute. You're being careful aren't you, darlin?"

"Always, love. I have a good looking young Colonel here that watches out for me."

"Hmmmm, wanna trade jobs for awhile? Here's Charley, take care and give my best to your Colonel."

"Bye, Mona," laughed Bronski. "Hi, Charley."

"Hi, Joe, how's it going?"

"Not good, we've had another explosion and two corporals have been killed. Mona is rounding up Gutterman, Bender, Walls, and Brennan for you to fly down this afternoon. They'll be dressed like first lieutenants. I want them to stay in the plane out of sight until it's dark. Corporal Lind will pick them up with their orders. I'll brief you after you get here, and by the way, you're invited to the General's house for dinner, casual wear. In the meantime have Mona run a check on Colonel James Leer, and three other colonels,

Colonel James Fertig, Colonel Richard Burton, and Colonel Ralph Evans."

"Sounds like you've got your teeth into something. I'll turn this over to Mona and see you about 1700 hours."

"CHAPTER EIGHT"

The big King Air settled gently on the runway, rolled out, turned, and continued off the runway to the parking area following the jeep with the "Follow Me" sign on the rear.

When the props stopped turning, Bronski and Hart approached the left side of the plane. The door opened and the steps dropped down. Charley appeared in the doorway. and came down the stairs grinning.

"Hello, you two boy scouts, have you earned your sleuthing badges yet?"

Bronski grinned as they shook hands. "No, were working on our 'Sneaky Pete' badges. Is your cargo safely secured?"

"All secured, partially briefed, and ready to go. You sure pick the best when you want help."

Bronski reached over and placed an arm around Charley' shoulder. "I assume that you're referring to my present company, also?"

"Flattery will get you anywhere, when do we eat?"

"The General said 1800 hours. We've got thirty minutes to brief you and wash our hands," laughed Hart, "the old boy is a stickler for prompt."

Mrs. Harris greeted them at the door. Hart introduced Bronski and Blake.

"Hello, boys. What can I get you to drink?"

Bronski asked for a bourbon on the rocks and Hart a martini.

Blake grinned. "I'd like an Old Fashioned Manhattan," he said, thinking he was throwing her a curve.

They stepped up to the bar while Emily went behind and deftly mixed their drinks. Blake and Bronski were impressed.

Hart smiled, he had been there before and was quite familiar with Emily's talents.

He lifted his drink. "To the most beautiful and talented bartender in the Army."

The others lifted their glasses. "Hear! Hear!"

Blake's grin faded when he lifted his drink and tasted the best old fashioned Manhattan he'd ever had. Hart laughed at his look. "I forgot to mention, Charley, that Emily is a world renowned bartender. Among the military population she is know as the 'Merlin Behind The Bar', in the best circles that is. She can mix drinks that you have probably never heard of."

Blake reached over, took her hand, and kissed it. "Please accept my apologies, dear lady, I was so overcome with your beauty that I failed to notice I was in the presence of 'Genius'."

"Bret Hart, where ever did you find such a delightfully charming young man as this?" she said, batting her eyelashes at Charley.

"Oh, brother," moaned Bret, "have you ever met such a pair as these, Joe?"

Emily and Charley burst out laughing.

Still laughing she led them out to the patio where the General, deck out in a hat and apron that read, "Best Damn Cook In The Yard", was tending steaks on the grill.

"Welcome, Gentlemen," he greeted them, "how do your like your steaks? I know it's medium rare for you, Bret."

"Same for me," said Bronski.

"Make mine rare, Sir," said Blake.

Bronski introduced him.

"General, this is Major Charley Blake, the office man and genius of our team."

"Good to meet you, Major, but tonight it's George and Charley."

"Fine with me, George."

"What was all the laughing about?" he asked.

"Darling, I have just met the most delightfully charming young man in the world, I'm never going to wash my hand ever again."

"I'm not going to touch that with a ten foot pole." The men joined her in a fit of laughter.

Bronski filled the General in on what they were going to do with the four operatives, and the investigation Mona was running on the four colonels.

"I hate to think that anyone of my officers would be capable of doing anything like this, but I guess it's a case of everyone being under suspicion, including me. Just don't tell Emily what you find out about me."

Emily laughed. "Don't worry, dear, I know all about your little escapades. I've just been patiently waiting for your to grow out of them. Only a stupid woman thinks her man is perfect."

The General laughed. "Now you can see why I love her. You didn't bring Mona with you by chance did you, Charley?"

"No, George, I've got her too busy doing work for Joe." He turned to Emily. "If you want to know anything about your husband, Emily, just call Mona and give her a few minutes, she'll give you all the dope on him."

The General turned a little red.

"Sorry, George, but in a case like this we have to be thorough, everybody is under suspicion. We even have a file on Emily."

Emily laughed. "I'll have to get friendly with Mona to make sure she doesn't show it to anyone. I'd be awfully embarrassed if the truth about my infidelity came to life."

"I'll bet that's some kind of infidelity," laughed Bronski.

"CHAPTER NINE"

Pvt. Lind picked up the four agents as soon as it was dark and handed them their orders. Gutterman was placed in logistics, Bender to ordnance, Brennan to communications, and Walls to Col. Leer.

The officers in charge had been briefed and threatened with hanging if they revealed a word of what was going on. None of them knew about the other. It was to be the slickest cover up not on record.

Bronski let three days lapse before he gave the go ahead for the transfer of the aides. There was plenty of griping by the colonels at first, but the agents were so efficient at their jobs that the complaints soon became smiles.

Col. Fertig soon fell under suspicion when the investigation revealed that he had served as armament officer at two other bases. Bender was assigned to Fertig, so he kept him under close scrutiny during his waking hours.

Bender reported to Bronski. "I'll put my money on this guy, Joe, he admitted to me that he had been an armament officer, but by putting a few innocent questions to him, I found that he doesn't know anything about the latest developments in explosives or remote detonating. I can tell he's pretty nervous about his own tail, but I'll keep an eye on him."

Gutterman was assigned to Col. Burton in logistics. Burton was tall, blond bushy hair, which he kept styled, handsome features, and a good physical build. He fancied himself quite a ladies' man. He was a good officer, however, and knew his job well. Gutterman was an excellent operative, so acting as an aide was a piece of cake. He anticipated Burton's every need. This pleased and impressed Burton and he confided in Gutterman, telling him about his clandestine meetings and torrid affairs with some of the ladies on the base. Confidentially, he told Gutterman he wasn't interested in ever becoming a general. The rank of colonel had a more romantic dash to it," he explained.

Gutterman reported to Bronski. "This guy is a good officer, Joe, he really knows his job and works hard so he gives the impression he's bucking for a promotion, but he's more interested in his love life than his is in a promotion. He tries to keep his love affairs secretive, but he's about as subtle as an elephant walking through a drum factory. Of course, he may be trying to cover up by giving me a snow job, but I doubt it very much. If he's guilty, he'll make a slip and I'll be there."

Bronski, Blake, and Hart sat down and went over the situation as it stood. "I'm beginning to think we're barking up the wrong tree, but we haven't heard from Brennan and Walls hasn't been assigned to Leer yet. We'll wait for a report from him when that takes place."

Brennan finally gave his report to Bronski.. "I'm afraid there's not much I can tell you about this fellow, Joe, all he knows is radios and communications. I'm surprised he ever made colonel. I doubt if he even knows how to strike a match correctly. But then sometimes stupidity can be a cover up for genius."

"Well, keep an eye on him and we'll just have to wait and see."

"CHAPTER TEN"

Three days later Bronski, Hart, and Blake walked into the motor pool. "Come look at this, Captain," said Ward.

Every car in the garage had a charge of plastic explosive in the trunk. Peel and Ward had removed the detonators and disarmed them. One car had the explosive but no detonator.

"Jesus H. Christ!" exclaimed Bronski, "what the hell is he trying to do, commit mass murder? Move those detonators away from the others and let's see who comes after the cars."

The first driver that showed up was Gen. Hoyt's. He signed for the car and drove out. Bronski, Hart, Peel, and Toro followed him.

"Take over, Charley."

They followed at a safe distance until they came to the corner of the street where Gen. Hoyt lived. They parked about fifty feet back from the corner. A jeep with two MP's passed the corner and headed in the direction of Hoyt's house.

"Pull up to the corner, Lind, and let's see what happens."

Bronski had put one of the detonators in a metal container. They saw the jeep was just about to the next corner and as the General's car pulled away from the curb, the detonator activated.

"Catch that jeep!" Bronski hollered at Lind. Two blocks away they overtook the jeep.

Bronski and Hart jumped out of the car with guns drawn and ordered the MP's out of the jeep. Toro sniffed around the vehicle and the MP's, and came up blank. Bronski patted the MP's and searched the vehicle but found nothing.

"Sorry, men, a detonator went off just as you passed the General's car and we thought it was you."

"No, Sir, I reported in on the radio just after we passed the General's car, but I don't see how that could activate anything," said the sergeant.

"OK, Sergeant, I'd appreciate it if you didn't mention this to anyone."

"No, Sir, mum's the word, Sir."

Back in the car, Bronski said to Hart, "Well, that shot that theory all to hell. I would have sworn it was them that triggered that detonator. Let's go back to the motor pool."

When they drove in, Sgt. Krase was standing by his jeep. "Good morning, Sir. You haven't by chance seen my partner, Corp. Wells, any place?" he asked.

"No, we haven't Sergeant."

"He was supposed to be here an hour ago."

"When did you see him last?"

"Last night, I told him exactly what time to meet me here."

One of the motor pool men let out a yell from the grease pit. "Holy shit! Come here quick."

They all ran over to see what he was hollering about. He pointed down in the pit. Corp. Wells and a black private, Ed Jones, were lying in the bottom of the pit. Wells had a knife sticking out of his neck and his lifeless eyes were staring up at them.

Bronski swore. "Son-of-a-bitch, this has all got to tie together somehow. This bastard has to be stopped. Lind, go call Col. Hansen and tell him I want him down here right away." Ten minutes later Hansen showed up and five minutes behind him Gen. Harris.

When he saw Bronski he said, "Christ Almighty, Bronski, when is this all going to stop? Hansen told me there were two more murders down here."

"That's not all, General, we found plastic explosives in every one of the vehicles in the garage this morning and detonators in all but one. We followed Hoyt's car after his driver picked it up. We had one of the detonators in a metal box. As soon as they got in the car and drove off the detonator was triggered. We thought we had the culprit, but we drew a blank. We're missing something here but I haven't been able to put my finger on it yet."

"Do you need more help? If you do, get it, the FBI or anyone else. I'll back you all the way."

"No, General, more help would only tend to dirty up the

waters and drive our culprit or culprits into hiding. Excuse me, Sir, I have to get to a phone. Come on, Hart."

At Col. Hansen's office, Bronski turned on the scrambler and called his office.

"Hi, Mona, Joe here."

"Hi, Joe, how are you doing?"

"Fine, Mona, but we're not making much headway with this thing. We've got a real pie here this morning, the two sergeants, Peel and Ward, with their dogs, found plastic explosive in every one of the vehicles. There was a detonator in all but one of them."

"Yipes! Whose car didn't have the detonator in it?"

"It wasn't assigned to anyone. That's not all, one of the MP's, Corp. Wells, and a black private, named Jones, were murdered this morning. The same M.O. as used on Corp. Davis who was killed last week, stabbed to death. Whoever did it is an expert with a blade."

He told Mona about the episode with Gen. Hoyt's car and the MP's.

"I'm overlooking something here, Mona, it keeps banging me the head, but I can't figure it out. Have you found out anything?"

"Yes, just came in this morning. They've located the black-market dealer that brought in the plastic and they're bringing him in for questioning. Call me back about 1400 or 1500 hours and I'll probably have the information for you."

"OK, Mona, I'll check back with you then." He flipped off the scrambler and turned to Hart. "We've got one break, they found the black-market dealer that brought in the plastic and are bringing him in for questioning. We'll know more when I check with Mona this afternoon."

"Do you think they'll find out who bought the stuff?"

"If I know Peek and Ringo, they'll find out, they're pretty good at interrogating."

"Get pretty rough, do they?"

"When they have to."

"You know, Joe, I've felt pretty useless following you around, but I've been mulling this situation over in my mind and like you, I feel like maybe we're shooting at the wrong ducks. Could these detonators be triggered by any other means than by these RELR12 units?"

"Hmmmm," murmered Bronski, "you may have something there, Bret, but I don't know what it would be. Let's call the office again, we may have just the man that can answer that for us."

Bronski turned on the scrambler back on and called the office. "Hi, Mona, Joe again, is Doc around?"

"Hello, Joe, we have to stop meeting like this, people are going to start talking. As for your question, yes, he's standing right here."

"Hello, Joe, what can I do for you except sing your praises to Mona?" (He ducked as she took a playful swing at him.)

"Doc, can you jump in a plane and come down here right away?"

"Sure thing, Joe, I'll see if Mona has anything for you and be on my way."

"Thanks, Doc, we'll meet you at the air strip. So long." He broke the connection and turned off the scrambler, then turned to Bret. "Doc is an electronics wizard, Bret, if anyone can tell us how these detonators are triggered, he can. Let's go gather up those we took out of the vehicles so he can look at them." They headed for the garage.

Charley met them when they got there. "Find out anything?" he asked.

"Yes, they found one black-market dealer that had the plastic shipped in. Ringo and Peek are bringing him in for questioning. I'm also having Doc fly down and take a look at these detonators. Bret thinks they may be triggered by some other means than the RELR12's."

.Sergeant Ward walked up with Raz. "Sergeant, we want to gather up all those detonators we found this morning."

"I have some and Sgt. Krase picked up some. He said he was taking them to Col. Hansen's office."

Bronski made a bee line for Krase who had a bag with the detonators inside. "Who the hell told you to pick those up?" he demanded, as he jerked the bag out of Krase's hand.

"Well, er, ah, no one," he stammered, "I was just going to take them to Col. Hansen's office."

"In the future, keep your damn hands off of things unless you're told or I'll have you digging latrines for the next twenty years. Do you understand me?" bellowed Bronski.

"Yes, Sir," he replied as he backed out the door.

He turned to Ward. "In the future, Sergeant, don't let anyone touch anything, even if you have to shoot the son-of-a-bitch. I'm serious."

Ward smiled. "Yes, Sir."

"Let's keep these separated. I don't know if Krase did anything to them but let's not take any chances." He looked around. "Who took the car that didn't have the detonator in it?"

The dispatcher was standing nearby and heard Bronski ask about the car. He picked up his clip board. "That was Corp. Kenelly, Sir, Col. Leer's driver."

"Did he ask for that one specifically?"

"No, Sir, he just went over to it and asked, "will this one be OK?" I nodded and he signed for it."

"Charley, Bret, let's go, I want to know why he picked up that particular car."

They found the car in front of the headquarters building with Corp. Kenelly standing alongside smiling. He came to attention as they walked up and stopped. He saluted Bronski.

"Did you pick up this car at the motor pool this morning, Corporal?" asked Bronski.

"Yes, Sir, is something wrong, Sir?"

"Why this particular car?"

"Col. Leer said to get a Chevy with air conditioning in it because we would be driving around the base. He said he thought there was only one Chevy with air conditioning in it, Sir," he answered, plainly nervous.

"Relax, Corporal, is Col. Leer in his office?"

"Yes, Sir, I think so, he should be coming out any minute, Sir."

"Thank you, Corporal, we'll check."

They reached Leer's office just as he was coming out.

"Good morning, Gentlemen," he said with a smile.

"Good morning, Colonel. do you have a minute? We have a couple of questions."

He opened the door again. "Very well, Gentlemen, come in."

"You sent your driver for a car this morning. Why did you specify that particular car?" asked Bronski.

"I told Corp. Kenelly to get one with air conditioning, because we would be driving around he base."

"But you specified a Chevy with air conditioning. Why, Colonel, it isn't that hot out."

He squirmed. "So I like air conditioning."

"You never used a car with air conditioning before, even on hot days." said Bronski, staring at Leer.

"Am I under suspicion or something?"

"Even your mother is under suspicion, Colonel, so don't get up tight. Until we find out who is responsible for all these bombings and murders, everybody is under suspicion, so calm down. You'll do better to cooperate with us."

"Very well," he replied. "It's just that I'm not use to being looked on with suspicion, I have always held positions of trust where ever I've served."

"All right, Colonel, sorry to have taken up your time."

When they got back to the car Bronski said to Hart, "Might be interesting to find out what positions he did hold at other bases. I'll have Mona check. Let's go over to Hansen's office and I'll give her a call.

Bronski turned on the scrambler and dialed the office.

number.

"Hi, Mona, Joe again."

"I warned you about this, Joe, but I really don't mind. What can I do for you this time, sweet?"

"I hate to pile work on you, but since I have Charley here I'll have to have you do it."

"Charley would give it to me anyhow, so what do you need?"

"You have a report on Col. Leer, see what you can find out about him from the other bases where he was stationed, anything about him personally, you know what I'm after. I'll check back with you later today. Thanks, love."

Bronski hung up the phone, switched off the scrambler, and turned to Hart. Lets pick up Charley and go have lunch. By then it will be time to go to the air strip."

"CHAPTER ELEVEN"

While they were waiting at the air strip they compared notes. Bronski filled Charley in on what they had done and learned, and Charley, since he was handling the investigation of the murders, clued them in on what he had accomplished to this point, which was very little.

"There's one piece of evidence I find at each blast site that I can't identify and it bothers me," said Bronski.

The Beech Baron circled over the air strip then made its approach for landing.

"That's Doc, he's an old fighter pilot and he always makes his approaches that way."

The plane touched down gently on the runway and taxied over to the "Follow Me" jeep that led him to the parking tarmac. The ground man jumped out of the jeep and indicated the tie down spot. Doc expertly swung the big plane into the position and stopped. At the signal from the ground crewman he chopped the engines.

"That's Doc," laughed Bronski, "puts it right on the dime every time."

As the slightly graying slim-figured man in his early forties jumped down off the wing, Bronski greeted him with his hand extended and a big grin.

"Hi, Doc, slick approach and landing as usual."

He laughed. "I have to stay in practice so you won't outshine me. Hello, Joe, good to see you. I hear you're in trouble as usual."

"Bronski laughed. "Meet Col. Bret Hart. Bret, Col. Doc Nagle."

"Good to know you, Colonel. I hope you don't get demoted for hanging around this maverick. We've got good reports about you from our spy source."

"Thanks, Colonel, you also come highly recommended," he replied grinning.

"How's this guy doing, Charley, is he earning his pay?"

"Between him and Bret, they're digging all the worms out of the woodwork. I think they're on the right track now, that's why they've sent for you, to dig out the last worm."

"Let's go sit in the car so we can talk," suggested Bronski.

Once in the car, Bronski handed Doc two detonators, one from each bag.

"Do you see any difference in these, Doc?"

He examined each carefully. "Yes, do you see this little disc under the connector of this one?"

"Yes."

"This one can be set off by a radio transmitter, this one without the disc can't. That little disc is a frequency selector. Something new out of Germany. We've got a couple of companies trying to duplicate them. It can be set to any radio frequency and triggered when the radio on that frequency transmits."

"God damn it Bret, I knew we were missing something, you hit it on the head when you asked if these could be triggered by any other means than by an RELR emote.
We've been working on the assumption that these blasts were set off by the remote. I'll bet if we check the frequency on one of those MP jeep radios it will trigger one of these detonators. That's what I couldn't identify, that little piece of metal I kept finding."

"Don't feel bad, Joe, only an electronics man who was familiar with these things would have caught it, they're too new."

"I think I'll have Mona run another check on Krase and see if he's ever had any electronics experience. You want to give her a call, Charley?"

"Will do, Joe, you've been using Hansen's phone, haven't you?"

"Right, it has a scrambler."

"Mind if I make a suggestion?" asked Doc.

"No, not at all, what's on your mind?"

"Why don't we borrow one of those jeeps tonight an see if we can trigger one of those detonators by transmitting on their radio frequency?"

"Excellent idea, Doc, we'll do it after dinner, about 2000 hours. We can go out to the parade grounds and no one will know what we're doing."

At ten p.m., the four of them went to the motor pool. Selecting one of the jeep, Col. Hart informed the sergeant on duty that they wanted to borrow a jeep for awhile and he would be responsible for it personally.

They drove out to the parade grounds. Bronski placed six of the detonators in a metal box, but disarmed them. Three had the little electronic devices and three without.

Bronski stopped the jeep and got out, removed one of the detonators that had the frequency selector attached, then walked out about a hundred feet from the jeep. He placed the detonator on the ground and returned to the jeep. Doc turned on the radio and pressed the mic key. The detonator was triggered.

Bronski took out another detonator, this time one without the frequency selector, and took it out to where he had placed the first one. He returned to the jeep. Doc turned on the radio and pressed the mic key again. Nothing happened.

They repeated this with all the detonators, obtaining the same results.

"There's you answer to how the blasts are being set off," said Doc, "now all you have to do is catch the culprit. You'll have to make sure you find the explosive before the car leaves the motor pool."

"I'll have Peel and Ward alter shifts around the clock," said Bronski.

"CHAPTER TWELVE"

The next afternoon Bronski put in a call to Mona.

"Hi, Mona, Joe here."

"Hi, love, I have something for you. We ran a pretty thorough check on Leer and Krase. Everyone describes Leer as a quiet congenial man, not a rank hungry officer. They almost had to beg him to take the promotion to colonel. They describe him as smart and exceptionally good at his job, honest as the sun. Lost his wife and daughter in a hit and run accident. Doesn't sound much like your man, does it?

"Got about the same story on Krase. Certainly not the MP type and from what they tell me he wouldn't know an electron from a glass eye," said Mona.

"I'm beginning to wonder if they're the same two guys. I think we should run some finger print checks. I'll get a sample of each and send them to you for comparison."

"We also got some information from the dealer that brought in the plastic. He brought in two cases, 220 pounds each. It was sold to Manfried Von Hoffer. We're running the name through and I'll get back to you as soon as I have something," added Mona.

"Thanks, Mona, I'll talk to you later."

"Bye, Joe, take care of yourself."

Bronski briefed the others on the information Mona had given him.

"Those descriptions sure don't fit Leer and Krase," said Hart, "I think you have the right idea about the finger print check. I'll get a set from personnel, but I think we should get a fresh set from each of them."

"Good thinking, Bret, let's find out when Krase goes to the NCO Club to eat. We can get Ward or Peel to go there and pick up a cup or glass that he's used. We can catch Leer at the "O Club" and get his. In the meantime we have to come up with a plan to catch the MP's that are setting of fthe blasts."

41

"I think I may have an idea, Joe, let me run this by you fellows," said Hart. "Suppose Peel and Ward play possum and let someone put a charge in one of the cars, then we'll sneak the detonator out of it before the car leaves the garage. We can arrange it so only one of the generals has a car that day. There are a couple of old cars that we are about to get rid of so we can take one of them, put a light charge in it, then place it down the street from the General's house. We'll have another car with three men that we can trust waiting at the next corner. If the jeep goes by and the decoy car explodes, we can nail them.

"We'll have to let the General in on it and hope he isn't the guilty one. We'll have Gen. Harris tell the others that he'll send a car for them at 1000 hours for a meeting in his office and to stay home until they're picked up. I think Hoyt would be the best one to take into our confidence. How does that sound?"

"I think that will work great, but I think we should wait a couple of days just to throw them off," said Bronski.

Charley had some information on the murder investigation. "Whoever wielded the knife that killed those three is trained in commando tactics. That wasn't just a thrust of the knife, the killer knew just where to inflict the wound so it would be fatal on the first thrust. Also it was a seven inch blade which indicates it was a combat knife."

"I don't suppose anyone would be carrying around a knife like that so you could see it, and I would imagine it would be difficult to run down all the men with that kind of combat training," reflected Bronski.

"Ahem," coughed Hart, "I don't recall you saying this was going to be easy." He had his tongue in his cheek suppressing a smile.

Bronski laughed. "Touche!" he said with a grin. "Let's go to work then."

"CHAPTER THIRTEEN"

Hart obtained a copy of finger prints for Leer and Krase from personnel without arousing suspicion. Charley had to get back to the office so he tucked them in his brief case, cranked up the King Air, and headed for Fort Clark, OSI headquarters.

Just as Bronski and Hart were about to leave the air strip, a corporal pulled up alongside the car and handed him a message from communications. It was from Mona, asking him to call the office. He and Hart headed for Hansen's office and the telephone.

Bronski turned on the scrambler and dialed the office number.

"Hi, Mona, Joe here."

"Hi, Joe, I haven't heard from you for a couple of days and I was afraid you'd found someone else," she said laughing.

Bronski smiled. "You know I could never find anyone to take your place, sweetie. Charley took off with those finger prints for you to compare."

"In the meantime I'll see if I can get a copy of their prints that I'm sure are on file at Fort Lewis," said Mona.

"Alright, we'll try to get some fresh prints as soon as we can and rush them to you. I'll check with you later."

"Right, bye, Joe."

He turned to Hart. " Let's hit the 'O Club' and see if we can catch Leer. Maybe we'll get lucky and get a good set of prints."

At the 'O Club' they stopped at the bar for a coke and held a light conversation. Bronski went to the mess officer. "When Leer comes in, keep a table next to him for us, but don't say anything."

"No prblem, Sir, consider it done."

Twenty minutes later Leer came in and went directly to the dining room. They could see him from where they were sitting and when they figured he was just about finished eating they signaled to the mess officer that they were ready for their table.

When they sat down Leer raised his head with a surprised look on his face.

"Good afternoon, Sir, how was your lunch?"

"Hello, Captain, it was fine, thank you."

"I talked to a friend of mine at Fort Lewis the other day and he said he knew you. He told me about you losing your wife and daughter. Sorry to hear that, how did it happen?"

Leer turned red and got nervous. "Fever, but they went fast. If you'll excuse me, I have an appointment." He got up and hurried out.

"That lying son-of-a-bitch, Leer's wife and daughter were killed by a hit-and-run driver." Bronski swore.

Hart took out a handkerchief and a plastic bag then placed the glass and cup that Leer had been using inside the bag.

"Good," said Bronski, "now we'll find out who this bastard really is. I hope the boys have been as lucky with Krase."

When they left the "O Club" Ward met them outside with Raz. He had a big grin on his face. He handed Bronski a plastic bag with a cup and glass in it.

"Jack-pot, Sir, he was holding them with both hands. Should get a good set of prints from both of them."

"Good work, Ward, now let's go over to Hansen's office and see if we can lift them off. I know he has the equipment there."

At the Security Office, Bronski lifted off perfect sets of prints from the cups and glasses of both Leer and Krase.

"Great!" exclaimed Bronski, "I think we should jump in the plane and take these to the office ourselves. The boys can cover things here." To Ward he said, "You know what to do, Ward, you and Peel take care of things and we'll be back in the morning."

"Don't worry, Sir, we'll take care of things, won't we, Raz?" The dog looked up at him and wagged his tail.

"I think I'd better go with you , Sir, and have Raz check out the plane before you get in it."

"Good thinking, Ward, let's go."

At the air strip Ward took Raz to the plane and had him check it inside and out. About the same time a couple of MP's in a jeep pulled up.

"Oh, oh, I'd better nip this in the bud, right now," said Hart. He walked over to the jeep. "Good afternoon, Gentlemen. I think I left my brief case at the security office, would you run back and get it for me?"

"Yes, Sir, be right back."

Hart returned to Bronski. "I sent them on a wild goose chase. They won't be transmitting on that radio, I disabled the antenna without them knowing it. We'd better get going."

Bronski laughed, "You sly fox, you."

Ward called from the plane. He handed Bronski a package.

"A little going away present for you, Sir, Raz found it under the seat. Here's the kicker." He handed him the detonator.

Bronski disarmed it. "Good work, Raz. Let's confuse them, we'll stick it back in when we return, but it won't go off. If they check it again they'll think they forgot to arm it or it's defective."

CHAPTER FOURTEEN

When they walked into the office, Bronski introduced Hart to Mona..

"Now I know why you call the office so much," he said as he took Mona's hand and held it.

"If I'd known you had such a handsome partner, I would have delivered all of your messages personally," smiled Mona. Hart blushed.

"Pay no attention to her, Bret, she gets dazzled every time she sees a uniform. Is Charley in, Mona?"

"In his office, Joe. Nice meeting you, Colonel." She gave Bret one of her best smiles.

"It's Bret, mam, I feel like we're old friends," he said smiling.

"Bret it is. Then you knock off that mam stuff," she said with a laugh.

Charley got up as they walked into his office. "Hi, Joe." They all shook hands. "Welcome to the office, Bret, now you'll see how the other half lives."

Bronski produced the new sets of prints and Charley pulled out a folder marked "Operation Boom". Hart smiled at the nomenclature when he read it. They visually compared these with the prints they received from Fort Lewis.

"Looks like we've got two new players. I'll send these over to the experts and let them run them down to see who they really belong to. When do you figure to put Bret's plan into action?"

"As soon as we get back we'll brief Gen. Harris so he can put his roll into play, then brief Gen. Hoyt as to what's going to happen so he won't have a heart attack when the bomb goes off in the decoy car. Makes it easy now that we know how they set off the explosions," said Bronski.

"When the jeep tries to get away, the other car, with the men I picked, will cut them off and cover them until we get there," explained Hart.

46

"Where did you get this genius, Joe?" Mind if I come along and watch the show?" laughed Charley.

"Not at all, that's a good idea, you could command the intercept car."

"Great, when are you going back?"

"In the morning, early."

"Good, I'll follow you in the King Air."

Peel met them at the air strip the next morning.

"We've got the decoy car all set up and the one that Gen. Hoyt will used picked out. Colonel, if you can have one of your men at the garage before daylight, we can have him drive the decoy over and park it down the street from Gen. Hoyt's house."

"Good work boys. I'll take care of it, that will be Sgt. Jer Johnson."

"CHAPTER FIFTEEN"

Bronski, Blake, and Hart met with Gen. Harris and briefed him on the plan, then contacted Gen. Hoyt, clueing him in on what was going to happen, also assuring him that he would be in no danger.

At 0415 hours, Krase showed up at the motor pool. Ward and Peel pretended they were checking out a car in the rear of the garage, but had him in view all the time. They watched as he opened the trunk of the General's car and place the explosive inside. When they were sure he had left they opened the trunk and removed the explosive. They reduced it to about one eighth then placed it in the decoy car with the detonator disarmed. Hart's man, also hiding in the rear of the garage, drove it to Gen. Hoyt's house then parked it about a hundred feet down the street. He armed the detonator then joined the others in the intercept car and waited.

At 0700 the General's driver came for the car. Ward and Raz pretended to check it out and the driver left. Ward, Peel, and the dogs got in another car and followed at a safe distance.

Bronski, Hart, and two more men had positioned their car so that they could watch for the General's car and the MP's when they showed. Ward and Peel parked behind at a discreet distance.

The driver pulled up in front of the house and as soon as Gen. Hoyt saw the jeep coming, left the house and went to the car. He and his driver stood by the car pretending to have a conversation until the jeep was just about opposite the decoy car, then got in. At that moment the decoy car exploded. The jeep started to speed away but Blake and his men pulled out to block the way then jumped out of the car with guns drawn.

The two MP's started to get out of the car, but changed their minds and raised their hands.

"What the hell is this?" demanded the MP Sergeant.

"Suppose you tell us." snapped Blake.

"I don't know what you're talking about."

Bronski and Hart pulled up behind them, got out with Ward, Peel, and two other men

"Start talking," snapped Bronski.

"About what," sneered the Sergeant.

"Alright, we'll do it the hard way." He set a charge on the hood with a dummy detonator in it. "If either of you get out of the jeep I'll shoot you. Now, the rest of you move back. There's a radio in that car back there on the same frequency as yours. When everyone is clear, I'm going to call you on it unless you start talking."

"The Corporal jumped out of the jeep. "For Christ sakes, wait, I'll tell you what you want to know."

The Sergeant started to draw his gun, but Bronski raised his. "Let's see how fast you are with that thing before I blow you away." He raised his hands. "OK, get out," ordered Bronski, "you men take their guns and cuff him. All right Corporal, start talking."

"Krase is running the deal and he threatens to harm our families if we don't do as he says. I'm not sure but I think Col. Leer gives him his orders. Krase murdered the two corporals and the black guy in the garage. He killed Davis, too."

"Get on your radio and call him. Tell him to meet you at the motor pool as soon as possible."

"Jeez, not with that thing on the hood."

Bronski pulled the detonator out. "It's a dud, now call."

The Corporal keyed the mic nervously and called Krase.

"Unit three calling unit one."

"Unit one, over."

"This is unit three, meet me at the motor pool as soon as possible. We got-----."

Bronski grabbed the mic. "You want to get your head blown off?" He turned to the others. "Cuff this guy, too, and bring the jeep We'll go to the motor pool. He's probably warned Krase."

As they turned the corner to the motor pool, Krase was

speeding towards the main gate. The guards had been warned not to let anyone through without a signed pass from Bronski, so when they saw Krase speeding towards them they opened fire on the jeep. A tire blew and it went out of control then flipped over.

Bronski and Hart, with two men in one car, and Blake with three men in the other, pulled up and stopped.

"Good work," said Bronski to the guards, "let's see if this joker is dead or just hurt."

Hart got to him first. "He's alive, just dazed."

"Throw him in the car and we'll take him to the stockade, then we'll see if our men have Leer in custody."

When they walked into Security they could hear Leer demanding to know what this was all about and to be released immediately. His face fell when he saw Krase being shoved towards him in handcuffs.

"Will someone show me the courtesy of telling me what's going on?" he demanded.

Bronski grabbed him by the front of his coat and shoved him into a chair. "Suppose you tell us, Leer, or whatever your name is?"

"What do you mean by that?" he sneered.

"Let me call my office and we may find out," said Blake.

"Here use this phone," said Hansen eagerly, "it has a scrambler."

Blake turned on the scrambler and dialed the office.

"Hello, Office of special Investigations," answered Mona.

"Hello, Mona, Charley here. Getting pretty formal, aren't we?"

"Have to show a little class around here once in awhile so I don't get out of practice. What can I do for you, dear?"

"Did you get the results back on those prints yet?"

"Sure did, love, looks like Joe got himself a real pair of class act skunks. The so-called Col. Leer is Herr Manfried Von Hoffer, top Nazi assassin and bund organizer. The phony Sgt. Krase is Karl Krausmann, also

50

a top Nazi assassin. They must have killed the real Col. Leer and Sgt. Krase. We've got a couple of agents trying to track it down now. Can you nab them?"

"We can do better than that, we have them both in custody. Thanks, Mona, I'll talk to you later." He hung up the phone and turned off the scrambler.

"Well, Joe, and Bret, you bagged a couple of biggies. Our friendly Col. Leer is Manfried Van Hoffer, top Nazi assassin. The good Sgt. Krase, is Karl Krausmann, also a top Nazi assassin."

He looked at Von Hoffer. "Colonel, huh, you smelled phony the first time I met you. Throw them in the stockade and we'll question them later. Let's lean on that Corporal and see if we can find out who else is involved in this mess."

They took the Corporal in a side room and sat him in a chair in the middle of the floor.

"You can make this easy on yourself or we can do it the hard way. Who else is involved in this?"

The Corporal sat silent.

"We're running out of patience, fella," snapped Bronski.

Two of the men that Hart had enlisted to help them, M/Sgt. Sandy MacMillan and M/Sgt. Pat Boone, spoke up.

"Mind if we try, Sir."

"OK, try."

They jerked the Corporal out of the chair. Each took and arm and began to raise them up to his shoulders behind his back. when it seemed they would be pulled out of the sockets he screamed with pain. After a few minutes they eased off.

"Ready to talk?"

Silence-------.

They raised his arms again, this time higher. He really screamed now. They held the pressure, increasing it more and more. He sobbed and begged for mercy.

"Ready to talk or do we keep going?"

"No, no, I'll talk." They released him. "Promise me you'll protect my family."

They sat him in a chair.

"OK, let's hear it," said Bronski.

He was sobbing so hard he couldn't talk so Bronski stood waiting patiently. Finally he began to name names. All but four of the MP's were involved, and one corporal in the motor pool.

"Krase made us do it. He said if we didn't cooperate his organization would torture our families. We didn't know anyone was going to get killed. He told us we were just going to blow the engines and put a scare in the generals. When Gen. Trackwell and Smith got killed he told us we were all involved and wouldn't let us back out. Today was the first time I was involved in an explosion, and when that car went up I was scared to death."

"All right," said Bronski, "I've got it all down, so lock him up. Now all we have to do is find out why and who is behind it all. I have an idea that only Hoffer and Krausmann can tell us that. Let's work on Krausmann first, but let's put them in separate rooms with two guards with them. We'll instruct the guards that they are not to talk to them, no matter what they say or do. If they get too hard to handle, we'll instruct the guards to shoot them in the leg."

Bronski sent six men to bring out the prisoners one at a time. When they were stowed in separate rooms, he sent two guards back to guard the cell block.

"Since we have them stewing for awhile, we should go report to Gen. Harris and let him know what's happened," suggested Hart.

"I think you're right, do you want to come along, Charley?"

"No, I think I'd better stay here and make sure nothing goes wrong. As soon as you get back I think we should round up the others."

"OK, we won't be long."

Lt. Fitch announced their arrival, and the General waved them in. "God damn it, it's about time you two are getting here.   Hoyt told me what happened this morning and I've been on pins and needles waiting to hear the details from you two."

"Sorry, General, but we've been pretty busy," replied Bronski.

"I heard you had Leer in custody, what's the story?"

"Sir, your Chief of Staff is not Col. Leer, he's Manfried Von Hoffer, a Nazi assassin and bund organizer," said Bronski.

Between him and Hart, they related what happened and how they trapped the MP's, Leer, and Krase.

"We don't have the compete story yet, but we will when we get it out of Hoffer or Krausmann. They'll be tough nuts to crack so we may have to use some drastic methods, but be assured, one of them will talk and we'll get the whole story."

Back at Security, Blake suggested they work on Krausmann first.   "He's the weaker of the two and if we can get him to talk, Hoffer will sing."

"Come on, Sandy," said Hart, "we're going to question Krausmann."

"OK,   squarehead, "   said Bronski, "we want some answers and we want them fast."

"Got to hell, I ain't telling you anything."

Mac and Boone moved over alongside of him.   "The Captain said he wanted some answers,   did you understand him?"

"Fuck you."

Mac gave him a chop on the back of the neck and he went down on his knees. "Watch your language, Hinie."

"What and who's behind this?" asked Bronski.

"I don't know what you're talking about."

"I think you do, now talk or I won't be responsible for what Sgt. MacMillian does."

Krausmann spit in Bronski's face.

Bronski's temper

flared and he hit the German in the face, knocking him off his feet.

With his mouth and nose bleeding, Mac and Boone jerked him to his feet.

"Do that again and it will be the last time you ever spit. Now answer my questions before I really get mean."

Krausmann remained silent. Mac drew back his boot and kicked Krausmann in the knee. The bone snapped and he let out a scream. The two sergeants held him up.

"You've got one more knee and two elbows, plus I learned a lot of tricks from your kind during the war," said Mac.

Still he kept quiet except for his moaning from the pain.

"Have it your way," said Mac, and he drew back his boot and kicked Krausmann in the other knee.

Krausmann screamed. "No, no, please, I'll tell you what you want to know."

"That's better," said Bronski, "now, what's this all about and who's behind it?"

"This is a plan by the Nazi Party to demoralize your Army. It was to happen at three of your bases."

"Where?" demanded Bronski.

"Here, Fort Ritter, and Fort MacKenzie. We put someone like Von Hoffer in and eliminate your generals until he is in command, then our agents move in and take over the top positions and eliminate all your top officers. Von Hoffer has a list of all our people at the other bases and our agents."

"When was all this suppose to happen at Ritter and MacKenzie?"

"After we had taken over here."

"OK, leave him here under guard and we'll go to work on Hoffer," said Bronski.

"What about my legs?"

"You'll live until we get back to you. You Nazis are good at·inflicting pain, but you can't take it, can you? Right now we have more important things to do." To Hart and Blake he said, "Let's go round up the rest of this miserable gang before we work on Hoffer, they might get wind of what's going on and take a powder."

"Good idea, let's take Mac and Boone with us," suggested Hart.

They rounded up six MP's and a corporal at the motor pool.

"If we hadn't broken this thing they would have had their own army within the U.S. These are just the flunkies that Krausmann forced to work for him. It'll be interesting to know what he has on some of these guys and what he threatened to do to their families. We can get that out of them later. Soon as we get them to the stockade, we can go to work on Hoffer," said Bronski.

"I think we can get him to talk if you'll let us, Sir. We spent some time in the Orient. Those people are experts at loosening up a tongue," said Mac.

"OK, we'll ask the questions, you get the answers," laughed Bronski.

After the prisoners were safely tucked away, they went to the room where Hoffer was. Mac excused himself. "I'll be back in about ten minutes, Sir."

"OK, we'll wait for you."

When Mac came back he was carrying a satchel. "I'll be ready in a minute, Sir."

"Since we know you're not a colonel, you won't need these." He reached over and ripped off his eagles and medals. "Take the blouse off, too, you disgrace it."

He started to object, but Mac and Boone jerked him to his feet and tore the coat off. Bronski ripped off his collar insignias, tearing his shirt in the process.

"You won't need these either, so sit down at the table."

Mac shoved him into a chair and began taking things out of his satchel. On the table he laid a hammer, two large nails, two lengths of rawhide, a large wad of cotton, and an oversized combat knife which he stuck in the sheath on his belt. They all looked at the assortment with curiosity.

He pounded the nails in the table about six inches apart and bent them over halfway, then tied one end of a rawhide to one. He grabbed Hoffer's wrist and tied the other one around it tight. He then tied the wrist to one nail and fastened the end to the other nail. Boone held his left arm tight.

"What's going on, why are you tying my hand down like that, and why did you tie my wrist so tight?" he demanded. "I tied your hand down so you wouldn't move it and I tied your wrist so you wouldn't bleed to death when I start chopping off your fingers for not answering the Captain's questions."

"Ha!" Hoffer sneered at him, "You Americans are too soft for that."

"Start asking, Captain." He pulled the knife out of the sheath.

"We know what your plan is, Hoffer, so now we want the names of your conspirators at Fort Ritter and Fort MacKenzie. We also want the names of all your agents."

"I don't know what you're talking about," he sneered.

Mac brought the knife down with deadly accuracy and took off the first joint of Hoffer's thumb.

He screamed and swore at Mac. "You crazy son-of-a-bitch!"

Mac brought the knife down again and took off the rest of the thumb. He screamed and swore again.

"Watch your language, Kraut, or I'll take off a few more fingers. Hart, Bronski, and Blake raised their eyebrows in surprise at Mac's actions.

"You can't do this, I don't know anything, I don't know what you're talking about," he wailed.

"I'm waiting for an answer," said Bronski.

He looked at his severed thumb, dumbfounded, not believing this. "You crazy son-of-a-bitch, you can't do this, I have my rights. I want a lawyer."

Bronski, Hart, and Blake could hardly believe Mac's actions, but they needed answers.

"That's only in civilian courts. This isn't a court, you have no rights here, none of us are even here. Now, you have nine more fingers to go, I'm waiting."

Mac raised the knife.

He started to object. "I don't-------.

Before he could get it out, Mac came down with the knife and took off the first joint of his index finger. He screamed again. "NO, NO, NO, I tell you!" He began to rattle off names of his counterparts at other bases and all the agents.

"Who are your contacts in the U.S. and who are your suppliers?"

Mac raised the knife threateningly, and he blurted out the names.

"Who are your superiors in Germany?"

"They will kill me if I tell you that!"

"You have a choice, you can tell us, and take your chances with them, or Mac can start chopping off your fingers."

He broke down and began sobbing, then he gave Bronski the names.

"Who has the rest of the explosives and other supplies?"

Hoffer gave him the names and where they were located..

"Where's the rest of your cache hidden?"

He started to say something , but Mac raised the knife and he changed his mind. "It's locked in the file cabinet in my office."

"Where's the key?"

"In my pocket."

Bronski removed the key and handed it to Blake. "Here, Charley, take a couple of men and go collect the stuff."

"Wait a minute, Sir, these monkeys are noted for booby trapping things, so let's find out." He raised the knife and Hoffer cringed. "Is the cabinet booby trapped?"

"Yes, but I didn't have time to arm it when they came after me."

"It had better be safe because if I hear one small pop, I'm going to start chopping one inch at a time and won't stop until I reach your ears. Do you believe me?"

"Ja, ja, you are crazy enough to do it."

As Blake was leaving, Bronski said, "You be damn careful opening that cabinet, you heard what he said."

"Yes, but with Mac's method of getting the truth, I believe him," laughed Blake. "I think we should have Mac and Boone transferred to our office to work with us, I like their methods."

"We might talk about that later, now be careful."

Blake returned with three boxes of KXG 76 plastic explosive, a case of detonators, and a box of eighty little frequency selector discs that Doc had discovered and showed them how they worked.

They weighted the explosive and estimated how much was used in the blasts, plus what they found in the vehicles in the motor pool. It totaled about one hundred pounds. Hoffer told them that four hundred pounds was all they received, but they had made arrangements to have another two hundred pounds shipped in. He finally gave them the date of the shipment, where it would be received, and who would receive it.

"Just in case you've given us any erroneous information, or not enough, Sgts. McMillan and Boone will be here to take care of you, because you're going to remain here until we have everyone, who's name you have given us, in custody or eliminated. Do you understand me? The trouble with you people is that you think we Americans are a soft and easy target. Well, think again, Buster. It took us awhile to uncover your little scheme, but as you can see, we're not as dumb as you think. Now, there's just one more thing you have to tell us, what did you do with the real Col. Leer and Sgt. Krase? I'm sure you killed both f them, but we want to know what you did with the bodies. They were good soldiers and we want to see that they're given a proper burial."

Hoffer told them how they had found out that Col. Leer and Sgt. Krase were to be transfered to Fort Rycker and when they were to leave. They were kidnapped at the airport as they were leaving, murdered, and their bodies hidden in a shallow grave. He gave them the location.

The files for Col. Leer and Sgt. Krase were sent to Fort Rycker from Fort Lewis, which included a copy of their finger prints. Hoffer had been unable to switch them until just before Bronski arrived. The original prints were later discovered in Hoffer's office.

For the next week, Bronski and Hart, who had been assigned by Gen. Harris to work with the Office of Special Investigations, Blake and twenty of their operatives, made up a team and swooped down on Fort Ritter and Fort MacKenzie with lightening speed. By the end of the week they had every one of the names that Hoffer had given them in custody, including their American contacts. All of the explosives and supplies were found and confiscated.

"CHAPTER SEVENTEEN"

Bronski and hart flew to Germany and presented their evidence to their German counterparts. The entire Nazi Party was rounded up and taken into custody. The German government gave them swift trials, and they were either executed or given sentences from several years to life, depending upon their involvement.

Bronski and Hart then returned home, satisfied that they had done a thorough job. The entire staff of the OSI was invited to Fort Rycker by Gen. Harris for a celebration dinner and special thanks for all the officers and men.

Bronski was promoted to Major, and Bret Hart was promoted to Brigadier General to fill the slot left vacant by the death of Gen. Trackwell. Gen. Harris appointed him Chief of Staff. Bronski, Hart, and Blake were awarded the Meritorious Service Medal.

Sgt. Peel, Sgt. Ward, and all the men that helped to resolve the plot were promoted. M/Sgt. MacMillan and M/Sgt. Boone were promoted to Sr. M/Sgts., By special authorization of the President of the United States. That rank not authorized for the Army.)

Mrs. Trackwell and Mrs. Willis were both there to personally thank Maj. Bronski, Brig. Gen. Hart, and Maj. Blake.

All during dinner, Mona and Emily had their heads together talking which made Gen. Harris very nervous. After dinner Mona put her arms around his neck, kissed his cheek, and whispered in his ear, "Don't worry, General, your secrets are safe with me." Emily stood off to one side, smiling. Actually she knew as much about her husband as Mona did. Gen. Harris smiled brightly and said to Bronski, "Now I know why you all love this girl."

Mona put her arms around Bronski. "Congratulations, love, this is the way I like us to meet. Too bad the Chief couldn't make it. Now if you'll excuse me, I'd like to spend some time with a brand new Brig. General."

Sgt. Peel and Ward came up to offer Bronski their congratulations and thanks.

"I think this calls for six steak dinners at the 'O Club', said Bronski.

Peel and Ward looked at each other then at Bronski.

"What do you mean, Sir?"

"You two, Hart, me, Toro, and Raz. Do you think the mess officer will object?" They all joined in a laugh.

"No, Sir, they both love steak, and I don't think anyone will argue with them."

The next day the mess officer welcomed them with a big smile. All the diners smiled as they watched Toro and Raz being served their steaks at the feet of their handlers.

"CHAPTER EIGHTEEN"

A military tribunal was convened at Fort Rycker for the purpose of bringing all the guilty parties, involved in the plot to assassinate the generals and take over the base, to trial, to wit, Herr Manfried Von Hoffer, Karl Krausmann, and all the men they had allegedly coerced into aiding them in their plot.

Military council was appointed for the defendants since no civilian attorney would accept the case.

The Court found all the parties guilty as charged. Von Hoffer and Krausmann were sentenced to be hanged. Their accomplices were all given dishonorable discharges from the service, and prison sentences of various lengths, depending upon their involvement.

Col. Frank Miner, Head of the OSI,
opened the folder on his desk, and smiled at the nomenclature.

Case identification, "Operation Boom", Fort Rycker, Ala. Details enclosed.

The case has been closed and all guilty parties have been apprehended, tried, and sentenced in accordance with their involvement.

Signed,

Joseph Bronski, Major, Special Investigator,
Office of Special Investigations
U.S. Army

JB:mf

Copies to:
George Harris, Lt. Gen. Commander, Fort Rycker
Bret Hart, Brig. Gen. Chief of Staff, Fort Rycker
One Each, All General Staff Officers, Fort Rycker

PART TWO

"Operation Sharp Shooter"

"OPERATION SHARP SHOOTER"

Col. Frank Miner, Chief of the Office of Special
Investigations, U.S.Army, entered his office at 0750 hours,
removed his jacket and sat down at his desk.

At 0755, his secretary, Mona Ferguson, opened his
door.

"Good morning, Frank, coffee?"

"Good morning, Mona, yes, please."

She brought her hand from behind her and produced a
steaming hot cup of coffee.

"Here you are, Chief, just as you like it, black and hot."

He smiled. Are you a mind reader, Mona, you always
seem to anticipate my thoughts."

She laughed, a sparkling laugh that seemed to light up
her face and the room. "No, Sir, show me a man that
doesn't like to start off his day with a nice fresh made cup
of coffee, and I'll show you a man that's a grump the rest
of the day."

Frank laughed. "Just seeing you laugh, Mona, is
enough to start my day off right."

The phone rang.

"I'll get it," he said as he reached for the instrument.
"Good morning, Col. Miner here."

"Good morning hell, Chief, Senator Slocum from South
Carolina has been murdered."

"When, where?" asked Miner.

"This morning, about 0600. He had just stepped out the
front door to get the paper and a bullet caught him between
the eyes. The killer must have had a silencer, no one
heard the shot. His wife got up about 0630 and went to
look for him. She found him on the front porch, dead."

"Where are you now?"

"I'm at the morgue. They're digging the slug out so I
can take it to the lab. The doc here is good, he says he
can tell us from how far away the shot was fired, as soon
as he finds out the caliber of the gun and the depth of
penetration. The way it looks to me, he got it just before
he bent down to pick up the paper."

"How'd you get the call?"

"Lt. Hendricks from Homicide called me, it being a senator."

"Get back to me when you have more information. In the meantime, I'll keep Blake available in case you need him.

"Right, Chief."

Joe Bronski, Major, Special Investigator, considered one of the best in his field, Five feet ten, stocky build, dark wavey hair, and deep hazel eyes that seemed to look right through you.

"Now why in the hell would anyone want to kill a nice man like Senator Slocum?" thought Bronski, as he mulled it over.

"CHAPTER TWO"

At 0900 hours the phone rang. Mona answered it.

"Good morning, OSI."

"Good morning, Miss Mona, this is Eddie Warren, Senator Slocum's assistant. May I speak with Col. Miner?"

"Of course, Eddie, hold on." She rang Col. Miner's phone.

"Eddie Warren, Senator Slocum's assistant is on the line, Chief."

"I wonder what that pansy wants?" He punch the button for line one.

"Good morning, Eddie, what can I do for you?"

"Col. Miner, I thought you should know that the Senator received a threatening letter last week. He was supporting the gun ban bill, you know."

"What did the letter say, Eddie?"

"I think I should bring it over to you, Sir."

"Alright, Eddie, you do that. You haven't got your fingerprints all over it, have you?"

"Oh, no, Sir, I've been holding by the corners like they do on TV."

Miner rolled his eyes up. Good, Eddie, bring it over so we can take a look at it."

He hung up the phone. "I wonder where Slocum ever found him?" he said to himself

Twenty minutes later, Mona buzzed him. "Eddie Warren is here, Sir."

"Send him in, Mona, and bring your pad, I'd like you to note this conversation."

Eddie followed Mona in, holding a handkerchief with the letter and envelope wrapped in it.

He handed the handkerchief to Miner. "This is the way I see them handle things on TV so the fingerprints don't get smudge."

Mona suppressed a smile. Frank lowered his head and coughed. "That was very wise of you, Eddie. I'll send it down to the lab and see what they can find from it." He held the letter by the corners to impress Eddie and read it out loud.

"Senator Slocum,

Some very influential people do not want the gun ban bill passed. You are getting in the way. Back off or suffer the consequences."

The letter was typewritten but had no signature.

"Hmmmmm," mused Frank. "Someone is very interested in squelching those bills. I wonder who the very influential people are? Gives you food for thought. Here, Mona, call the lab and have Tony Tondini send someone for this. Thanks, Eddie, " he said as he stood up and extended his hand. "Keep me informed if you hear anything else."

He stood up and shook Frank's hand. "Yes, Sir, I will."

When he left Frank wiped off his hand. "Like shaking hands with a soft wet fish."

At 1155 hours the phone rang and Mona answered it.

"Good morning, OSI."

"Good morning hell, Mona, put the Chief on for me and stay on the line."

"Hold on, Joe, I'll ring him for you." She pushed the intercom button. "Joe is on the line, Frank, doesn't sound too happy."

Frank pushed the button for line one.

"Hi, Joe, what is it?"

"You tell me, Chief, Senator Sloan has just been murdered. Same MO, a slug right in the middle of the forehead. What the hell is this, shoot a senator week? Whoever the killer is he's a crack marksman. Uses a Remington or Winchester 308, and I assume a scope, silencer, and a 150 grain cartridge. The Doc says he was at least 300 yards away when he shot Slocum. I'm going to need Charley on these. Tell him to meet me at Sloan's residence. Lt. Hendricks has cordoned off the entire block around Slocum's house and is doing the same at Sloan's. Tell Charley to hurry, I'm going to need his help."

"OK, Joe, I'll get him right away."

"Lt. Col. Charley Blake, Special Investigator, thirty one, five feet ten, one hundred eighty pounds, blond hair, slightly unruly, hazel eyes, handsome features, and an athlete's build. Joined the service in 1942 after completing law school. Completed basic training and went to Officers School at the same time Bronski was there. They became close friends. He was assigned to the Intelligence Division of the Army and decorated many timed for his courage and service. He, too, was a top investigator.

"Christ, Charley, this guy has no heart, he shot Sloan right in front of his wife. She's still hystrical. Same MO shot right in the middle of the forehead as he turned to go to his car."

"We know which way the shot came from so let's go see what we can find about three hundred yards from here, then we can question some of the neighbors. There are only four houses in that direction," said Blake.

They stepped off three hundred yards and searched.

"Look here," said Bronski, picking up an object in the grass, "an empty shell. 308, one hundred fifty grain. That confirms what the Doc told me. The killer must have been in a hurry to have left this. Now let's question the people in the two nearest houses."

At the first house, no one was home. "Looks like they haven't been home for awhile; the grass needs cutting," observed Blake, "let's try the one across the street."

A young maid answered the door. "Good morning," she said, smiling.

"Good morning, Miss, I'm Major Bronski and this is Lt. Col. Blake." They showed her their ID's. We're from the Office of Special Investigations. Did you happen to hear a shot this morning, or see anything suspicious over there by that big tree?"

"No, sir, I didn't hear any shot, but I did see a van parked over there when I got up at 5:30."

"Can you describe it?"

"Yes, it was light blue, I think it was a Chevy."

"Did you happen to notice the lisence plate?"

"As a matter of fact I did, it had something yellow on it, shaped like a state or something. Two of the numbers were 3 and 6. It looked pretty new."

"Could it have been the state of Florida? They have that on their license plates."

"Why yes, I'm sure that was it. I didn't recognize it, but now that you mentioned it, I'm sure it was Florida."

"Was there anything else about the van that you noticed?"

"Let me see, oh yes, the windows were real dark and there was something sticking out of the top. It looked like one of those periscopes they have on submarines."

"Thank you very much, Miss, you've been very helpful. Would you mind giving us your name?"

"Not at all, it's Marie Hallorin. I'm the maid here."

Bronski wrote her name in his book.

"Is there a phone where we can reach you in case we want to know anything else?"

"Yes, it's 972-3334. this is Senator Egan's house."

"Very good, and thank you again, Miss."

"You're welcome. Good-bye, and good luck."

As they left Bronski said, "Well, that gives us something to work on. Let's measure the distance from where we found the shell to where Sloan fell."

"I've got a hundred foot tape in the car, I'll get it," said Blake, as he hurried off.

The distance measured three hundred yards plus a few inches.

"I think we have all we need here; let's go to the morgue and see what the Doc can tell us."

At the morgue, Doc Caleb gave them the same story on Senator Sloan as he had on Senator Slocum.

"This man you're dealing with is diabolical, he plans his killings to the minute detail. I'm surprised you found that empty shell. I wouldn't be surprised if he came back looking for it. He plans his shots at exactly three hundred yards and hits his victims right in the middle of the forehead. a man that's that good a marksman surely is known somewhere. He's more than likely a veteran. Here's the slug, I'm sure it will match the other one."

"Thanks, but I hope we don't see you again," laughed Bronski.ess.

Doc laughed. "in your business, it's inevitable."

"Let's visit Sloan's office and see if his secretary can tell us anything."

Senator Sloan's office was in an uproar over the news of his death. After dealing with several hysterical women, they finally located Sloan's secretary, Miss Perkins.

"Tell us, Miss Perkins, has the Senator received any threatening letters lately?" asked Bronski.

"Yes, it's on his desk, come with me."

They followed her into Senator Sloan's office and she started to reach for the letter.

"Don't touch it, Miss Perkins, there might be fingerprints on it that we can lift off."

Bronski picked up the letter by the corners and read it. He handed it to Blake, who took it by the corners.

"It's a duplicate of the one sent to Senator Slocum. Do you have a large envelope I can slip this in?"

She went to her desk and returned with a 10 X 13 manila envelope in which he slipped the letter.

"I don't suppose he saved the envelope?"

She went around the desk and opened a drawer. "As a matter of fact, he did." she picked it up by the corner and offered it to Bronski. He smiled and opened the big envelope so she could drop it in.

"I take it the Senator was backing the gun ban bills," said Blake.

"Yes, he was very much in favor of them."

"Well, thank you, Miss Perkins, this will help."

"Somebody sure as hell doesn't want those gun ban bills to go through," ventured Blake.

"It might help if we could figure out who would benefit most by having them thrown out, other than the NRA."

"I can't see any value in those bills myself. If a criminal wants a gun he'll get one from an illegal dealer. The only way they're going to cut down on crimes committed with guns is to make the punishment so severe that a guy will think three time before using one. It's our judicial system that need overhauling and judges who aren't afraid to hand out the death penaty," said Blake.

"I tend to agree with you. Now, why don't you see what you can run down on the van and I'll see what I can find out about the gun."

CHAPTER THREE

Blake went back to the office and had Mona dial the number for the Florida DMV.

"Good afternoon, this is the Florida Department of Motor Vehicles?"

"Please hold for a minute, I have Col. Blake on the line to talk to you."

"This is Col. Blake, of the Office of Special Investigations. I need some information on a vehicle,"

"Yes, Colonel, how can I help you?"

"I'm looking for a light blue van, believed to be a Chevrolet, with Florida plates, two of the numbers are 3 and 6. "

"It will take me awhile to get this for you, Colonel, can I call you back?"

"How long would a while be?"

"Anywhere from a half to an hour, no longer."

"It's imperative that I get this information as soon as possible. I'll stay on the line until you get it."

"Very well, I'll do my best." Blake heard him lay the phone down and say, "Don't let anyone touch this phone or they'll be on the unemployed list." Blake smiled.

He laid the phone on the desk, took a sheet of paper and with a felt tipped pen printed. "DO NOT TOUCH THIS PHONE, OR ELSE!" then signed it, W. Gibbons. He turned to two girls. "Millie, Edie, I want a list of all the Chevy vans with a three and a six in the license plate number. I have a Colonel waiting on the line for the information, so shake it."

Twenty nine minutes later he picked up the phone. "Col. Blake, I have the information you want."

"Very good, shoot, what is it?"

"There are twelve Chevy vans with a three and a six in the license plate number. Here is a list of the names and addresses."

He read off the list to Blake.

"Thank you very much, Mr. er, er?"

"Gibbons, Sir, W. Gibbons."

"Yes, Gibbons, thank you very much, Mr. Gibbons, you've been extremely helpful and I appreciate your cooperation."

"Glad to have been of service, Sir, any time."

Bronski checked the Winchester Arms Co., in New Haven, Conn. for their model 308, to find out many of that particular model were made. They gave him the number that were made, serial numbers, and the names of the distributors to whom they had been sold.

His next step was to contact the distributors and find out which dealers received which serial numbers. Assuming that the killer purchased the gun someplace in the east. he checked only the dealers located in the eastern states. From these he obtained the name and address of the purchasers.

Bronski now had to run down the purchasers and check their weapons for ballistics. So far he had a list of seven distributors in the east, to which seventy-three guns had bee sold. Several operatives were helping him gather this information.

Blake started their Florida operatives on the list he received from the Florida DMV, of vans with three and six in their license plate numbers.

After an intense search their results were as follows: out of twenty two vans, only five were light blue. One was owned by an elderly widow, one by a girl at the Florida State College, one had been totaled in a collision, one by an older couple that were vacationing in Arizona, and one by a Vitorio Casselli. The license number was LFE-36M. The address turned out to be that of his girlfriend's house, Sylvia Herron.

When two investigators knocked on her door and asked for Vitorio Casselli, they were greeted with a string of swear words.

"That dirty son-of-a-bitch, he talked me into co-signing for that fucking van and now the no good bastard ran out on me. I'm stuck with the fucking payments and I don't even have the fucking van. I hope when you find him you shoot the son-of-a-bitch."

"Would you happen to know where he is now?"

"Shit, if I knew where the bastard was I'd go shoot him myself."

"Here's my card," said the investigator, "would you call me if you hear from him or about where he is?"

"Gladly, Major."

"Whew!" exclaimed Jack Dix, "That is one pissed off mama. We'd better call Blake and let him know what we found out." He dialed the number of the office.

"Hello, OSI."

"Hello, Mona, Jack Dix, is Charley around?"

"Yes, Jack, I'll ring him for you."

"Hello, Jack, what's up?"

"Hello, Charley, we've got some good news for you. We got the license number if the van; it's LFE-36M. The ourchaser's name is Vitorio Casselli. His address is that of his girlfriend. He talked her into co-signing for the van and now she's stuck for the payments. Boy, talk about mad. I left my card with her and she said she'd call me if she heard from him."

"Good work, Jack, stay with it and let me know the minute you find out where this guy is. In the meantime I'll see what we can find out about him."

Bronski's men were busy checking out the gun distributors.

74

"CHAPTER FOUR"

The following morning the phone rang in Frank's office just as Mona was setting a fresh hot cup of coffee in front of him. She picked up the phone. "Good morning, OSI."

"Good morning Mona, is the Chief in yet?"

"Hi, Joe, yes, he's right here. I hope you have some good news for him."

"Sorry, no, Mona, there's been another murder."

"Yee Gods, here's Frank'"

"Hello, Joe, what now?"

"Senator Koslowski got it this morning. Same MO, just as he came out the door, right in the middle of the forehead. I called Charley, he's going to meet me there."

"Damn!" exclaimed Frank, "I wonder who's going to be next? We'd better get word to these senators to take precautions. Wasn't he pushing the gun ban bills, too?"

""I'm pretty sure he was. We'd better warn all the backers. Can you take care of that, Frank?"

"Yes, get back to me after you check this one out."

"Right, talk to you later."

Bronski and Blake checked out the Koslowski residence and the area around it. They found he same thing they had found at the other murder scenes. One of the neighbors had seen a light blue van parked about three hundred yards from the Koslowski residence, but again, no one heard any shots.

A light blue van was parked about three hundred yards from the low ranch style house where Senator Egan and his wife Ellen lived when he was in Washington. The van appeared to be unoccupied because the dark tinted windows obscured anyone inside. It was therefore impossible to see the figure crouched inside peering through the low profile periscope that protruded through the roof. The van had been parked in other locations along the street where the occupant could observe Senator Egan's movements.

The Senator had been warned to use extreme caution when leaving the house, especially in the morning. If he saw a light blue van he was to get back in the house immediately and call one of two numbers given to him, Homicide or OSI.

"Senator Egan started out the door to go to his car when he saw the light blue van. He quickly jumped back through the door and into the house. At the same time, something struck the door jam. He went directly to the phone and dialed one of the numbers he had been instructed to call.

In less than five minutes a patrol car with two uniformed officers, turned onto the street and stopped at the house. It was just two and one half minutes after the blue van sped away. The two officers got out and went up to the door.

"Good morning, sir," they said as Senator Egan opened the door, "we got a call to check out a blue van and to contact you. Are you all right, sir?"

"Yes, I'm all right, but you missed the blue van, it sped away just a couple of minutes ago. I didn't hear any shots but something hit the door frame just as I ducked back through the door. There," he pointed, "you can see the hole."

One of the officers examined the hole. "It looks like a bullet hole, Ed, we'd better get hold of Lt. Hendricks right away. Could we use your phone, sir?"

"Yes, right this way. He opened the door wider so they could enter.

The desk sergeant answered. "Fifth Precinct, Sgt. O'Malley."

"Hi, Sarge, Jim Riley here, get me Lt. Hendricks quick."

"Homicide, Lt. Hendricks."

"Hi, Lieutenant, Jim Riley. We're at Senator Egan's house. The killer fired a shot at him but missed and hit the door frame. Better send someone to dig it out, we'll wait."

"Stay right there and don't leave the Senator alone. Keep him away from the windows."

Fifteen minutes later Lt. Hendricks and two detectives showed up. Ten minutes after that Bronski and Blake arrived.

"Thank God you listened and were on the look out for that blue van," said Bronski, "did you notice anything special about the van, Senator?"

"Not really, when I saw it was light blue, I ducked back in the house. That's when I heard something hit the door jam. I quickly called the number I was given and a few minutes later these two officers arrived." He thought for a minute. "Now that I think of it, I seem to remember that the windows were real dark and there was something sticking out the top."

"That coincides with what Miss Hallorin told us, so I would say we're looking for the right van."

Lt. Hendricks dug out the slug and handed it to Bronski.

"Here you are, Joe, see if it matches the other three. Senator, I'm going to leave a couple of my men here to escort you to and from your office. Please don't go outside without them and remain in the house with the drapes drawn when they bring you home. I know this is an inconvenience but your life is in danger until we catch whoever is responsible for these killings."

"Very well, Lieutenant, I'm in your hands."

"I'll have two men here in about fifteen minutes," he said as he reached for the phone. "In the meantime, these two officers, Jim and Ed, will stay with you. Be sure to follow our instructions."

As they were leaving he said to Bronski, "I'll put out an APB on that Van and have every cop in the city looking for it."

"We'd better give this information to the State Police and have them do the same
we don't know where this guy is going next."

"I'll take care of it for you, Joe."

"CHAPTER FIVE"

When Blake got back to the office he had a message from Major Dix in Florida to call him as soon as he got in. His phone rang at the same time he was reading the message.

"Col. Blake here."

"Jack Dix, Charley."

"I just got through reading your message. Mona must have read it and put through the call as soon as she saw me come in."

"Charley, I had a call from Sylvia Herron, Vitorio Casselli's girlfriend. She said he sent her the money she's paid out for the van and enough to pay it off. He also sent her money to join him as soon as he finds a place. He's going to send her the address. She's still ticked at him so she's going to call me with the address when she gets it. She doesn't intend to meet him."

"Hmmmm, I wonder where he got so rich all of a sudden?"

"She didn't say except that she's sure he's mixed up in something crooked."

"OK, keep in touch with her and let me know as soon as she gets word where to meet him. Be sure to take care of her for her help."

"Will do, Charley, on both counts."

Vitorio Casselli was born six hours after his parents passed through Ellis Island, upon arriving from Sicily. His father, Anthony Casselli, was a cobbler and had been promised a job with his cousin who owned a shoe repair shop in Philadelphia. He was honest, hard working, and a fine craftsman who took pride in his work.

Angelina Casselli, Vitorio's mother, had been a seamstress in Palermo, Sicily, so Anthony's cousin put out the word and soon she had numerous customers. The word of her fine work spread quickly.

Vitorio was a bad apple from the time he was old enough to run the streets. He stole anything that wasn't nailed down.   His twelfth birthday he spent in the reform school for stealing hub caps.

Two years later he was back in the reform school for breaking into coin operated telephones, serving two years out of a three year sentence.   He broke parole and was picked up in a stolen car. His big mistake was stealing a car   that   belonged   to   a   police   sergeant. This brought him a six-year sentence, two of which he served in the reformatory and four in the State Prison.

Unfortunately his criminal education was enhanced by his association with hardened criminals. While in prison his behavior left a lot to be desire, so he was repeatedly turned down for parole, thus serving his full six years.

After his release he wound up in Florida and made connections with the mob through his prison associates.

Vitorio was handsome and had a glib tongue, which was how he managed to get together with Sylvia.

"CHAPTER SIX"

Thirty-six Model 308 Winchesters were sold to a distributor in South Hackensack, New Jersey, and then sold to six different dealers. Bronski and his men began to track them down. One dealer still had his original order of four, in stock. Another dealer had ordered six and sold three., He gave the agents the names and addresses of the purchasers and they set out to locate them.

A well to do sportsman purchased one. It was fired and the slug failed to match the ones taken from the dead senators and the one from Senator Egan's door frame.

The second one was purchased by an ironworker and had never been fired, he claimed. The slug from it was a mismatch.

The third was purchased by an elderly gentleman who was about to send it to his son in Colorado. It failed to match.

The third dealer had ordered seven and had six in stock, having sold one to a commercial fisherman who lived on his boat, the Mary Dee, anchored in Boston Harbor. The slug from his was also a mismatch.

A fourth dealer had ordered ten and sold them all to the New Jersey Gun Club. The owners were all asked to come out and fire a round into a sand bag so the slugs could be compared. None of them matched.

The fifth dealer had ordered three. Two were still in stock. One was sold to a police sergeant on the Boston Police Force. His failed to match.

The last dealer, The Silver State Arms, owned and operated by Dick Stadtmuller, had ordered six, sold two, and had deposits on the other four. He furnished the agentsa with the names and addresses of the two purchasers. The first one they tested belonged to a druggist; it failed to match.

Bronski was beginning to think they were barking up the wrong tree,

The last rifle was purchased by a mechanic, but his wife was deathly afraid of guns and made him get rid of it.

When questioned, he claimed he had sold it to a man who had come in to have some work done on his van. He found the bill for the work he performed, but had only a name, John Smith, and no address. Further questioning revealed that it was a light blue Chevy with Florida license plates, LFE-36M. Jackpot!

Bronski contacted all his agents. "See if you can run down anyone who has purchased 150 grain cartridges for a 308 in the past month and a half or two."

They found three people who had purchased shells for a 308, two with the purchase of their guns. The third was very adamant about wanting 150 grain ammunition. The dealer gave Bronski a good description of the purchaser. Six feet, about one ninety, blond hair, approximately thirty to thirty-five, and a livid scar down the left side of his face, apparently from a knife wound. Checking back with the mechanic, he verified the description.

A police artist sat down with the two men and made a composite drawing of the suspected killer. When they were satisfied with the accuracy of the drawing, copies were made and distributed to all law enforcement agencies in the eastern states. This was the one purchaser that specifically wanted 150 grain cartridges. The others wanted 180 and 195 grain bullets.

Three days later Blake got a call from Major Dix. He'd heard from Sylvia and had an address in Baltimore, Md., 1015 Lamont St. Blake immediately put a surveillance team to watching the house. The second night they hit pay dirt. Vitorio showed up and they took him into custody.

After twelve hours of grueling questioning, Vitorio still maintained he didn't know anything about any killings. He admitted he bought a van but claimed he sold it. When showed the Police Artist's picture he feigned innocence, claiming he had never seen the man.

"I know he's lying, Joe, but we can't shake him," said Blake.

"I think I know how we can get him to talk" smiled Bronski.

81

"What have you got in mind?"

"Remember the two sergeants at Fort Rycker, Mac and Boone?"

Blake threw back his head and laughed. "You sadistic son-of-a-gun."

"Hey, we've got lives at stake, this guy can give us some information so I say anything goes."

The light blue van cruised slowly around the block in a quiet residential area on the outskirt of Arlington. Arlington was the home away from home for a number of U.S. Senators and Congressmen. On this particular street was the home of Senator and Mrs. Wallace from the State of Michigan. It was seven o'clock in the evening. The Wallaces were just sitting down to dinner. The dining room was visible from the street, As the van passed the house it slowed down almost to a stop. The driver of the van was studying the house with a pair of binoculars.

Twice the van circled the block, each time slowing down almost to a stop in front of the house, the headlights dimmed. Inside the Wallaces were enjoying their dinner prepared by their cook, Honey Belle, unaware that they were being watched.

The following evening the blue van appeared again, at the same time, observing the Senator and his wife as they dined. The van with lights dimmed, circled the block three times, again slowing down almost to a stop in front of the house.

The third evening the blue van approached the house at the same time and slowed as it passed. The second time it came down the street and stopped just past the house. A rifle barrel protruded through the side window and there was a noiseless flash. At the same instant the Senator dropped his napkin and bent down to retrieve it. There was a crash as the window was shattered by the bullet that lodged itself in the wall behind the Senator's chair.

82

Mrs. Wallace screamed and the Senator raised up, confused by the shattered window and the noise of the bulltet striking the wall.

The van sped away, the driver not waiting to see if his bullet had found its mark. He saw the Senator bend down and it was so close to the moment he fired, he thought he had scored a hit.

Senator Wallace quickly went to the phone and called one of the two numbers that had been given to him. Within minutes two patrol cars pulled up to the house. Lt. Hendricks called OSI. The night operator quickly transferred the call to Major Bronski's apartment.

"Bronski here."

"Damn, Joe, our killer took a shot at Senator Wallace. Fortunately he missed this time. Wanna come down and take a look?"

"I'll be there in about thirty minutes." He hung up and dialed Lt. Col. Blake's number.

"Blake here.

"Joe, Charley, I'll pick you up in about ten minutes. Our killer took a shot at Senator Wallace but missed."

Mrs. Wallace answered the door when they arrived. They surveyed the damage and questioned he Senator.

"You're very lucky Senator, the man that fired at you is an expert marksmen, I can't figure out how he missed."

"I dropped my napkin on the floor and bent down to retrieve it. I heard the window break just as I bent over."

"I'd say that napkin saved your life," said Bronski, "he must have fired at the same moment you bent down. I'd suggest that you keep your drapes closed when you're in the house. I'm sure he'll try again when he finds out he missed you."

Lt. Hendricks dug the slug out of the wall. "It hit a stud otherwise it would have gone right through. Here you are, Joe, that makes a set of five for you."

"I don't have to take this to the lab. I'll make a bet it matches the other four."
"

"Senator," said Hendricks, "I'm placing two men out here around the clock until we catch this nut. They'll escort you to your office and home every day. Don't leave your office during the day unless they're with you. When you're home, keep your drapes closed and don't step out of the door unless they say it's OK."

"All right Lieutenant, what ever you say."

Every senator was warned and Bronski ordered guards for all the backers of the gun ban bill,

"CHAPTER SEVEN"

Bronski flipped the intercom switch on.

"Yes, Joe," answered Mona.

"Would you get Gen. Harris, at Fort Rycker, for me."

"Yes, love."

In a few minutes his line lit up.

"Gen. Harris' aide is on the line, Joe."

"This is Major Bronski, is Gen. Harris available?"

"This is Capt. Fitch, Major, I'll get the General for you right away."

"Major Bronski, how are you and what can I do for you?"

"I'm fine, Sir, and I need a favor."

"Just ask, young man, and if it's in my power, it's yours."

"I need to borrow a couple of you men for awhile."

"That's a simple request, who do you want?"

"Sr. M/Sgt. MacMillian and Sr. M/Sgt. Boone, are they available?"

"This whole base is available for you if you want it, Joe."

"Thanks, General, but all I need is Mac and Boone. Could you have Mac or Boone call me in a bit? I don't know how long I'll need them."

"They're yours for as long as you need them. I'll have Mac on the phone in a few minutes. They can be ready whenever you want them."

"I'll come pick them up, I can be there in about three hours. I'll be flying the King Air."

"I'll have Fitch connect you with Mac and they'll be waiting for you at the air strip. Good luck in whatever you're doing."

"Thanks, General, I'll tell you about it later."

Three hours later the big King Air eased into the traffic pattern at Fort Rycker and touched down on the runway. The "Follow Me" jeep was waiting for him to turn off and he tailed it to the parking Tarmac.

Two cars were sitting by the strip waiting when Bronski stepped out of the door and down the steps. General Harris and General Hart were standing beside them. He saluted the two generals.

"Hello, Joe, how are you?" asked Hart.

"I'm fine but we've got troubles, someone is shooting our senators that are backing the gun ban bills. We've got some leads but haven't been able to pin anyone down."

Hart smiled. "You must have some interrogating to do."

"Yes, we've got one that we haven't been able to get anything out of. He has the information we want but he won't talk. I thought I'd give Mac and Pat a crack at him ."

Hart laughed. "I'm sure they'll get you some results."

"I haven't heard any explosions," laughed Bronski, so I guess no one is after your job."

"No," laughed Hart, "I don't think anyone wants it, the General keeps me pretty busy."

"Here comes Mac and Pat. Say hello to your men for me and I'll keep in touch. Give my best to Emily, General."

"I will, Joe, she'll miss seeing you."

"Sometime later. Sir, I promise. I'll bring Mona, too."

Hart grinned.

He greeted Mac and Boone when they boarded the aircraft. Starting the engines, he taxied out to the runway and waved at the two generals as he took off.

"There goes one hell of a man," remarked Gen. Hart.

"Yes, I wish he were one of us here at Rycker," answered Gen. Harris.

In the air Bronski turned on course, climbed to altitude, then turned on the auto-pilot. He signalled for the two sergeants to join him in the cockpit, briefed them about the senators, gave them what information he had so far, and told them about Casselli.

"We're certain this Casselli is connected with the killer or knows who he is and where to find him but we haven't been able to get anything out of him."

"Got another Hoffer on your hands, haven't you, Major? We figured you wanted us for something like this so we came prepared. We've got everything we need."

Bronski smiled. "I figured you could get him to talk."

On the outskirt of Atlanta, Ga. a light blue van cruised down the street of an exclusive residential neighborhood. Four white colonial mansions were situated on this street. The largest of these was the home of Beauregard Hamilton, who was serving his sixth term as senator for the state of Georgia.

For three days the driver of the van had been carefully observing the house and studied the movements of the Senator.

It was Saturday morning. A white Mercedes pulled into the driveway, and Senator Hamilton emerged from the house carrying his golf clubs. The driver got out of the car, shook hands with the Senator, opened the trunk of the Mercedes, and placed the bag inside.

The van drove on past the house and stopped down the street. When the Mercedes pulled out of the driveway it turned in the opposite direction. The van made a U-turn in the street and followed at a discreet distance.

The Magnolia Country Club, an exclusive club for Atlanta's elite, was located about five miles outside of the city. A large wrought iron gate with a security guard was at the entrance. As the Mercedes approached, the guard activated the switch and the gate swung open. He touched the brim of his cap and waved them through. The driver and the others waved a greeting.

The van drove past and parked down the road in an obscure spot where there were bushes and trees for concealment. He was about three hundred yards from the putting green of the fourth hole.

From the rear seat he removed a case then ducked into the bushes where he would be undetected.

He opened the case and removed parts of a rifle and scope. Assembling these, he took three cartridges from his pocket, loaded the magazine, then sat back to wait.

About two hours passed before four men and their caddies approached the green. The gunman pulled his gloves on a little tighter and raised the scope to his eye. All four men were dress pretty much alike which confused the gunman as to which one was Senator Hamilton. All four had their backs to him. He picked out the Senator, placed the cross hairs on the back of his head and squeezed the trigger. Quickly he made his way out of the bushes back to his van and drove away.

On the fourth green, three men stared in disbelief as their companion pitched forward, blood flowing from where the top of his head had been.

"What the hell!" exclaimed the Senator, "did you hear a shot?"

"No! Who in the hell would want to kill Ed? I didn't think he had an enemy in the world," said one of them, looking down at their fallen friend.

Bronski and the two sergeants walked into the interrogating room. Blake and another agent, named Stevens, were with Casselli.

"Hello, Mac, Boone, glad to see you," greeted Blake. "We're not having too much luck with this fellow, he's got a bad memory."

"Maybe we can improve it a little," said Mac, setting his satchel on the table and removing its contents. Two large nails he pounded into the table and bent them over. To one he tied a rawhide thong. With another he tied Vitorio's wrist tight, then tied his hand to the two nails.

"Why are you doing this?" asked Vitorio, wide eyed.

"That's so you won't jerk your hand away when I start chopping off your fingers for not answering the Major's questions."

"You can't do this, it's against the law."

"So is killing senators."

"Who's killing senators."

"Who is killing the senators?" asked Bronski.

"I don't know nuthing about no killings."

Mac brought the knife down and took off the tip of Vitorio's thumb. He screamed and cursed Mac. Mac back handed him.

"You son-of-a-bitch, you're crazy."

Mac hit him again, drawing blood from his split lips.

"Answer the Major and tell the truth, I'm just getting warmed up," snapped Mac.

Vitorio's eyes grew wide as he looked at the knife in Mac's hand. He raised it as though to strike.

"OK, OK, His name is Stan Dombrowski, he paid me to buy a van for him."

"Is that where you got the money that you sent your girlfriend?"

"How'd you know about that, did she squeal to you?"

"Never mind, just answer the questions. Where can we find this Dombrowski?"

"I don't know."

Mac raised the knife.

"No, wait," he sobbed, "he stays with me when he's in town."

"Why is he killing the senators?"

"I don't know."

Mac brought the knife down and took off the first joint of his index finger.

He screamed and looked with horror at his severed thumb and finger. He struggled with Boone to get free but he held him tight.

Mac jammed a wad of cotton on his fingers to curtail the bleeding.

"You've got the rest of your fingers on that hand then we start on the other one. Now do you want to start talking?"

"You can't do this, I have my rights," he said sobbing.

"When you started working with a killer, you gave up your rights and now you're about to give up some finger to go with them," said Bronski.

Vitorio looked at him with terror in his eyes.

"OK, OK, all I know is that there's a lot of juice behind this and plenty of money. I don't know any names but Dombrowski seems to have an unlimited amount of cash."

Mac raised his knife.

"No, no, please," cried Vitorio, "that's all I know except that I did hear him on the phone say that he was going to pick off somebody at a rally but I don't know where it is."

"I'll put Mona on it, she'll find out where they're having a big gun rally," said Bronski. "Get the Doctor to look at that hand and then put him on ice. I'll be back in a little while." He strode from the room.

"Mona, there's suppose to be a big gun rally some place, do you think you could find out where it's going to be? It's urgent so let me know as soon as possible. I'll be in Charley's office."

Thirty minutes late the phone in Charley's office rang.

"Yes, Mona?" answered Charley.

"Put Joe on, Charley."

90

"I've got your information, Joe. There's going to be a big anti-gun rally at Berkeley University on Saturday. You know how those kids are. It's suppose to be a real banger, With about six speakers."

"Thanks, Mona, our sharp shooter is suppose to be going there. Call Milt Barry in San Francisco and tell him to meet me at the Oakland Airport tomorrow afternoon. We'll be in the King Air. Tell him to bring some men."

"Please be careful, Joe, this guy has got to be a psycho."

"Don't worry, Mona, I wouldn't want to break our little family here. Joe hung up. "You ready to go, Charley? I'll get Mac and Boone, they've earned a little vacation."

He came out of the office looking for the two sergeants. He found them drooling over Mona.

"Come on you two lovers, we've got work to do."

Mona laughed. "See you later, boys."

"Where to this time, Major?" asked Boone.

"How would you like a little California sunshine?"

"Great, is that where the rally is going to be?"

"Yes, at Berkeley University."

"That figures, those kids will use anything for an excuse to protest, whether they believe it or not."

"This is suppose to be a big one."

Bronski filed an IFR flight plan and was given a clearance direct Wichita Mid Continent, RON, (remain over night) with reservations at the Holiday Inn, then an 0600 take off, local time, direct to Oakland Metro.

Late that afternoon Bronski called Oakland Metro approach and was vectored to a straight in on runway 9R. He was handed off to the tower and cleared to land.

Milt Barry the agent in charge of the west coast operation, met them when they taxied into the parking tarmac and stopped. Bronski greeted him as he climbed out of the plane behind Mac and Boone.

"Hello, Milt, I see you got my message."

"All Mona said was, get every available man and meet you here."

"How many men did you get?"

"Eighteen, and I can get more from the military if you need them."

"With your eighteen and my two sergeants we should have enough. These are Sgts. MacMillian and Boone."

"What's the scoop, Joe?"

Bronski briefed Barry and his men on the situation.

"All we know is this nut is trying to kill everyone that is for the gun ban bill and we've been told he is going to hit this rally. What I want your men to do is secure everything within four hundred yards of the speakers' stand. Work in pairs and don't take any chances. He's an expert marksman and has been hitting his victims from about three hundred yards. He's hit three in the middle of the forehead and one in the back of the head. We don't know what he's going to do here, but our informant says he's going to hit it. He uses a silencer so you won't hear any shots."

"How reliable is your informant?" asked Barry.

Bronski laughed. "Mac and Boone convinced him to talk and if you ever watched their methods, you'd know our informant was telling the truth. I'll explain when we have more time."

When they reached the Berkeley campus the agents spread out to secure the area. Bronski, Blake, Barry, Mac, and Boone approached the platform. A wild looking character seemed to be doing the organizing so they approached him.

"Are you in charge of setting up this show?"

"Who wants to know?"

Bronski showed him his ID.

"Do you think you're going to stop us, man?"

"No, MAN, we're not going to stop you, we just want to keep you alive."

He laughed. "What the hell is that supposed to mean?"

"There' a killer out there that is trying to eliminate everyone who is fighting for the gun ban bill. We have men covering the area, but this guy is a trained killer and we don't know where he's going to be. Anyone that gets up on that platform to start preaching will be a target for him."

"You're shittin' me, man, with all these people around. who'd be crazy enough to try something like that?"

"This guy is so don't laugh, MAN."

"OK, do what you have to do, but stay out of our way."

Bronski turned away from him. "Stupid bastard. Let's stick around this speakers' stand and keep our eyes open."

The crowd swelled until the area was full of students and spectators with refreshments ready to make a picnic out of the affair. Beer coolers were everywhere and some could be seen smoking pot. Bronski shook his head.

The loud speaker came to life. The wild looking character with the weird hairdo was at the mic.

"Do we want guns?" he hollered.

"NO! NO!" roared the crowd.

Six people were on the platform ready to speak to the crowd. The first one stepped up to the mic.

He raised both arms. "Fellow American," he started his speech. The next instant he was spurting blood from the hole in his forehead and pitched forward to the platform. It took several seconds for the people on the platform to realize what had happened. Some of the other speakers ran to their fallen friend.

"Get off the stage!" bellowed Bronski.

One of them stood up. "He's been shot!" The words were no sooner out of his mouth when hole appeared in his forehead and he tumbled off the stage. Mac and Boone were dragging the others off the platform to the ground. "Keep down," yelled Mac. "It came from that direction, Major," he hollered, and pointed.

Suddenly there was gunfire from that direction. The crowd was screaming and running wild in all directions.

One of the agents spotted Bronski. "Over here, Joe! We didn't hear any shots, but we saw those two on the platform drop and spotted the guy with the rifle. He took off among those buildings."

"Did you see him well enough to get a description?"

"He's about six feet, maybe 200 pounds. He's dressed in jungle fatigues."

"Signal the others to join us, we'll fan out and see if we can spot him."

The other agents joined up and spread out to search the campus. When they got to the parking lot, Mac grabbed Bronski's arm and pointed.

"That looks like him getting in that red Corvette on the other side of the parking lot!"

"See if you can hit his tires."

The Corvette burned rubber and zig-zagged out of the parking area, making it to the street.

"Commandeer some cars and call for a couple of helicopters. Maybe we can keep an eye on him from the air."

Barry and some of the agents raced to where they had parked their cars and were soon stopping to pick up Bronski, Charley, Mac, and Boone.

"Two choppers are on the way!" hollered Barry.

In a few minutes one of the chopper pilots called.

"We've got a red Corvette speeding south on I80. Man, is he moving. There's too much traffic or we'd try to run him off the road."

Bronski grabbed the mic. "Don't do anything but keep him in sight. If you try to stop him we could lose him or some innocents could get hurt."

Chopper: "Looks like he's working his way to 580. You'd better catch him or you'll lose him once he gets in those hills."

Bronski: "How far ahead is he?"

Chopper: "About seven or eight miles but you're coming up fast. The traffic is slowing him down."

Bronski: "Keep us informed as to how close we're getting."

Chopper: "I'm creating a traffic problem up here in a clear area, the cars are beginning to jam up. The Corvette is at the rear of the traffic. I'm coming back to see where you are."

Silence-------

Chopper: You're coming up fast, the traffic is moving now and you're about a mile and a half behind him. You should be able to spot him after you make this next curve."

Bronski: "We've spotted him, keep an eye on him."

Chopper: "Oh, oh, he's turning south on a side road, do you see him?"

Bronski: "We've got him. Now we've lost him in the trees, can you see where he's going?"

Chopper: "It's a winding road, no way he can get off. He's hidden in the trees now. Pause-- "He didn't come out, he must have gotten out of the car but I don't see him."

Bronski: "OK, we're at the car."

Chopper: "There he is, heading east on foot through those trees. Oh, he's shooting at me. Did you hear those shots?"

Bronski: "We can't hear him, he's got a silencer on that rifle. Move out of range, he hits what he shoots at. We're going to spread out. We have a hand held unit so keep talking."

Chopper: "I saw his puff of smoke, he's about a hundred yards east of the road."

Bronski: "Try to keep him in sight."

He turned to Barry. "I want this guy alive, we have to find out who is behind this. Keep under cover as much as possible because all you'll see is a little smoke from his piece."

The twenty three men crept forward slowly through the trees.

Chopper: "There's an outcropping of rocks ahead and above you, he's holed up in there. He's got good cover, so be careful."

"Let Boone and me try to take him, Major, we've been in similar spots. As soon as we spot him we'll signal to give us some cover fire. We'll go in from two sides. He can't shoot both ways at once."

"Alright, signal when you're ready, I'll pass the word." Mac and Boone checked their pieces.

Bronski: "Chopper, can you give us a pinpoint position on this guy? Two of my men are going to try to take him from two sides."

Chopper: "Do you see that shear rock just below those two big pine?"

"Bronski: "OK, we've got them."

Chopper: "He's at the bottom of the shear and to the right. He's got a good position, you may have to starve him out. I'm getting low on fuel, I'll have to leave in about five, but I can be back in about twenty. Maybe you'd better hold off until I get back."

Bronski: "Go ahead, we'll keep him pinned down until you get back."

"We'll work up part way so we can reconnoiter and wait for the chopper to come back," said Mac. "Boone, I'll go up the left side and try to get to that clump of rocks up there. You go up the right side and I think you can get to that rock pile by the big tree. We'll be able to see each other and be in a good position to nail this guy. We'll be above him so there's a good chance he won't see us until the last second."

"OK, I'll signal when I'm in position," said Boone.

96

"Remember, men, we want him alive so we can get him to talk," said Bronski.

The two men grinned. "Yes Sir, Major, we'll bring him back alive."

Bronski smiled and the two sergeants began to work their way up the hill, swinging wide to gain their positions, but keeping out of sight of the gunman.

The chopper was back in twenty five minutes. Mac and Boone were in position. There was a puff of smoke from the rocks and one of the agents let out a yell.

"Son-of-a-bitch, he got me in the leg."

"There's Mac's signal," said Bronski, "let's give them some cover fire."

The agents opened up and bullets were ricocheting off the rocks all around the gunman. There was another puff of smoke and another agent yelled.

"Ed's hit pretty bad, Chief," another agent yelled.

"Try to get him down to the car and call for some help."

Two of the agents carried Ed down to the road while the one with the leg wound limped along behind. Two CHP cruisers had just pulled up.

"We were just about to come up and offer our help."

"They have everything pretty much under control, but Ed here has a pretty bad wound in his side and Chet has a hole in his leg. Do you have a first aid kit?"

The trooper grabbed the first aid kit out of the cruiser and started to treat the wound.

"We'd better rush him into town, he needs more help than I can give him with what I've got. Get him in the rear seat and one of you come with me."

"We'll all go, Chet needs taken care of, too." They helped Ed into the rear seat and Chet got in the front with the trooper.

"I'll stay here in case I can be of assistance," said the other trooper.

Mac and Boone had maneuvered into position. The gunman spotted Mac, swung his gun around, and began firing. Mac saw him swing and ducked behind the rocks. Boone took advantage of the diversion and moved in closer. The gunman anticipated this and turned his gun on Boone, firing just as he dropped out of sight.

Seeing him turn, Mac took aim and shot him in the right shoulder, causing him to drop his weapon. Boone peeked out and saw what happened. Before their quarry could recover, Boone and Mac both moved in and landed on him. He struggled, but a hard blow from Boone's big fist took all the fight out of him and he sat staring at them.

"Hey, Major," called Mac, "we've got your pigeon."

Barry called to his men. "Gather round boys, looks like the show's over. Go up and help the sergeants drag that rat down here."

They dragged their prisoner down the hill as roughly as they could. "Christ, take it easy, I've been shot."

"I don't see anyplace where you've been shot," said Mac and he slapped him on the shoulder.

"Yeow! You son-of-a-bitch!"

"You know they had a lovely funeral for the last guy that called me that. Did I hear you apologize?"

"Fucccc-" he never finished the word, Mac's big fist split his lips and the blood spurted.

"Was that to be an apology?"

Silence----

"I can't hear you." Mac raised his fist again.

"OK, OK, apology." he mumbled.

"Where can we take him that's private?" Bronski asked of Barry.

"Private but not secluded."

"OK, we'll take him to Oakland, put a plug in that shoulder, then take him back to Fort Clark. Mac and Boone are experts at getting answers out of reluctant prisoners."

The next afternoon Bronski set the big King Air down on the strip at Fort Clark. Blake had radioed ahead and a car was waiting for them.

Benson put out his hand. "congratulations, Joe, nice work."

"Thanks, but give the credit where it's due. Mac and Boone are the ones that really captured him."

Benson smiled. "Tell me about it, does he still have all of his fingers?"

Mac smiled. "We're saving them for later."

On the way to headquarters, Mac and Boone gave Benson all the details.

"How's he get the split lips?"

"I had to teach him not to use foul language."

Bronski led the way to the basement interrogating room.

They sat the prisoner down at the table and Boone held him while Mac took out his bag of tricks and set them on the table. He then tied His wrists to the nails in the table.

"What the hell are you doing?"

"Just getting ready for the Major to ask you some questions."

"Go to hell, I ain't answering any questions without my lawyer here."

"This isn't a formal questioning, you don't get a lawyer."

"I know my rights, I get a lawyer."

"Your rights? What do you think this is a court of law? This is question and answer time," said Mac.

He took out his big knife out of the sheath on his belt.

"OK, Major, we're ready."

'Alright, we'll start with, what's your name?"

Silence---

Mac raised the knife and brought it down before the gunman knew what was happening. The first joint of his index finger was severed.

He stared for a moment with his mouth open then let out a scream and struggled with Boone to get his other arm free. Boone held him tight.

"You bastard!" he yelled at Mac. Mac Backhanded him across the mouth.

"The Major asked your name?"

"Smith."

Mac raised the knife.

Alright, alright, Dombrowski."

"Who hired you, and what's behind all your killings?"

"What killings?"

Mac brought the knife down and Dombrowski stared in terror at his severed finger. He screamed a swore at Mac while struggling to get free from Boone. Mac jammed cotton on the bleeding finger.

"I didn't hear your answer," said Mac.

"OK, I don't like the gun ban bill."

Bronski started to stop Mac, but he was too late and the knife took off his thumb. He screamed and began to sob without control.

"Who hired you?" repeated Bronski.

"Honest, I don't know," he sobbed, "I only saw him once, but I don't know what his name is."

"How do you get your orders?"

"They're left in a locker at Grand Central Station, along with the money."

"What's the locker number and where's the key?"

"It's 107 and the key is in my pocket."

Mac dug the key out of his pocket and handed it to Bronski.

"Here, Charley, why don't you check it out when you're sure no one is watching and then keep an eye on it to see who shows."

"OK, done. I'll take Bender, Gutterman, Walls, and O'Neil with me."

"Good choice." He turned to Dombrowski. "Now, you, describe your contact."

He hesitated then looked at Mac. "He's tall, Italian, I'd say in his sixties, white hair, styled, a neat white mustache, and a sharp dresser. Carries a stick with a gold knob handle. I'm not sure but he could be a senator or a politician."

"We'll have Mona run this through her computer and see what she comes up with. What's Vitorio Casselli's part in this?"

"He's just a money hungry punk. He did some flunky work for me, no smarts."

"OK, Mac, Pat, patch him up and out him on ice, you know what to do with him. I'll be in my office."

"Hello, Joe, honey, I heard you were back, how'd you make out?"

"Hello, Mona, we caught our killer, now we have to find out who hired him. Here's some info, run it through your computer and see what you come up with. I'll be in my office. Send the boys in when they come up."

Thirty minutes later, Mac and Boone knocked on Bronski's door."

They stuck their heads in.

"Good work, boys, too bad we have to resort to such brutal methods, but I must say they're effective. Why don't you get us some coffee from across the hall while I make out these reports and a couple of phone calls? Did you pay your respects to Mona on your way in?"

They both grinned. "YES, SIR!"

Bronski smiled.

"CHAPTER ELEVEN"

A little over an hour later Mona tapped on the door and entered. She gave Mac and Boone a smile.

"I think you'll find this interesting, Joe," she said as she handed him a computer printout.

Bronski leaned back in his chair and began to read. He nodded when he finished.

"Very interesting," he looked at Mac and Pat, "it seems our man is a bigwig in the Mafia, Signore Giovanni Martinelli, know as the "Enforcer". I wonder who he takes his orders from?"

The phone rang.

"Bronski here."

"Hello, Joe, Charley. We've picked up a couple of pigeons and are bringing them in."

"Great, come on in and we'll meet you down stairs." Bronski relayed the information to Mac, Pat, and Mona.

Charley and the agents came in with two swarthy looking characters.

"Here's your scumbags, Joe, and here's the package they left in the locker."

"OK, Mac, Pat, stick them back in a room and we'll talk to them later."

Mac grinned. "Right, Major."

"Let's see what's in the package, Charley.

An envelope and ten packages of $100.00 bills, marked two thousand dollars on the wrappers. $20,000.00.

The envelope contained the names of two more senators. At ten grand a shot, this boy was doing all right. Of course Mac bankrupted his money finger. Let's bring those two hoods in and see what we can find out from them."

In the interrogating room, Mac had one of the hoods tied to the table and Boone was holding his other arm.

"Wassa idee, how come you tie me down like this?"

"We're going to play twenty questions with the Major. We got some answers from your sharp shooting friend and now you're going to give us some. Every time you don't answer a question, I cut off a finger, savvy?"

"He's a dead man, you bluff, I tell you nothing."

"We'll see," smiled Mac.

Bronski and Blake entered the room. The two gangsters glared at them.

"What's your name?" Bronski asked the one at the table.

"Go to hell."

Mac slapped him hard across the mouth, drawing blood.

"OK, Gino Farichi."

"Where can we find Martinelli?"

"How the fuck should I know?"

Mac brought the knife down and took off the first joint of his thumb. He yelled and started screaming in Italian. At the same time struggling with Boone.

Mac raised the knife again.

"The Major asked you a question, are you going to answer it?"

"Go fuck yourself, who the hell do you think you are?"

Mac brought the knife down again and took off the rest of his thumb.

"Mother of Christ," he screamed, "stop him!"

"Sure, just as soon as you answer my questions."

"You can't do this," he sobbed, thrashing around trying to get free of Boone's arm lock.

The other hood stood there staring. The other agents couldn't believe what they were seeing.

Mac raised his knife again. "The Major's waiting."

"Oh Christ, stop him, I'll tell you." He gave Bronski an address where Martinelli could be found.

"I'll take a couple of men and try to run him down," said Charley.

"Take plenty of help. I'll see what else I can get out of these two. He turned back to Farichi. "Who gives Martinelli his orders?"

"I don't know, one of the chiefs I guess. They don't tell me anything, I'm just one of the soldiers, I take my orders from Martinelli."

Bronski pointed to the other hood. "Get him over here and let's see what he can tell us."

The hood began struggling to stay away from the table.

"Please, no," he pleaded, "not that, I don't know anymore than he does, he's telling the truth, we're just flunkies." He kept struggling.

"Who are some of the big chiefs?" Bronski asked Farichi.

He hesitated. Mac raised the knife.

"Oh God, no, not that again, I'll tell you." Bronski took down the names he gave him.

"If they find out we talked, we're dead," he cried, tears in his eyes. He looked at his hand in disbelief.

"OK, fellas, put them on ice until later."

They were shoved into a windowless room that was bugged with a tape recorder.

"Let's see what they have to say to each other."

The phone in Bronski's office rang.

"Bronski here."

"Charley's on the line, Joe."

"Hello, Charley, how'd you make out?"

"We're at Martinelli's house, we've got a warrant. He's suppose to be home in an hour. We've got his houseman cooling his heels here so he can't warn anyone of our presence."

"Fine, Charley, I think we got all the information we could out of these two. We have them in a bugged room, we'll see if they talk to each other."

"Alright, I'll call you when we're ready to come in."

Later they listened to the tapes which didn't reveal anything of importance.

(Farichi: "These bastards are mean, Tony, they would have cut off all my fingers if I hadn't talked."

105

(Tony: "You shouldn't have talked Gino, they're going to kill you." (The Mafia)

(Farichi: "Don't tell me you big brave bastard, you were ready to sing an opera for them so don't tell me. You would have told them everything before that big sergeant took the first cut, you son-of-a-bitch. You were sobbing when they tried to pull you to the table. You can act big, you got all your fingers. If anybody asks me I'll tell them you sang, too, and then let's see how brave you act.")

"That's enough," said Bronski, I think they told us everything they know. We'll see what we can get out of this Martinelli when Charley brings him in."

Col. Miner sauntered into Bronski's office and eased himself into a chair opposite him.

"Hello, Joe, making any headway?"

"Yes, Chief, I'm just finishing up a report on what we've accomplished so far."

"Good, how're your sergeants doing? I understand they have a very unique way of getting information out of your suspects."

Bronski smiled. "Yes, they do, but we won't discuss it."

"That's good," said Miner, holding up his hands, "I don't want to know the details."

"Charly's out picking up the man that gives our killer his orders, and we have the names of those who supposedly give him his orders. We're narrowing it down, Chief. With any luck we should know pretty soon who's behind all of this. At least we don't have to worry about senators getting killed for awhile."

"Fine, keep me posted. Care for a cup of coffee?"

"Yes, I would."

He started to get up when Mona walked in with two cups of hot coffee.

"Here you are fellas, hot and black."

Miner stood up and started patting himself.

"What's the matter, Chief?" asked Bronski.

"I'll swear this girl has me bugged. She even knows what I'm thinking sometimes."

Bronski and Mona laughed.

"I know you both like your coffee and I just made a fresh pot so I figured you'd like a cup."

"But I just mentioned it to Joe."

"I know, I heard you, the intercom switch is on."

"I'll be damned. I'm glad I didn't say anything about you."

Mona smiled as she turned to the door. "That's all right, I know it would be something nice." She tossed her head and went out laughing.

Miner and Bronski shook their heads laughing.

"What would we do without her?" laughed Bronski.

Charley called. "We're on our way in, Mona, tell Joe."
"OK, will do." She rang Bronski's office. "Charley called, Joe, he's on his way in."
"Thanks, Mona, I'll meet him downstairs."

Bronski, Mac, and Boone met Charley when he entered the interrogating room with Martinelli and three more Mafia hoods.
"Hi, Joe, this is Martinelli and these three were with him so we brought them along so they couldn't spread the word that we picked him up."
"Good work, take them in the other room. Sit down Mr. Martinelli, we have a few questions for you."
"I don't say nothing without my lawyer."
"You're not in a court of law, this is the Office of Special Investigations for the Army."
"What's that got to do with me?"
"Just the fact that you've been paying Stan Dombrowski to kill some senators."
"You're crazy, you can't pin something like that on me."
"No? A couple of you go get Farichi."
They brought Farichi in. When Martinelli saw his right hand bandaged up his eyes opened wider.
"What happened to you?"
"The same thing that will happen to you if you don't answer my questions," said Bronski.
"That big son-of-a-bitch cut off my thumb."
Mac hit him in the mouth. "Do I hear an apology?"
"OK, ok, ok, apology."
Martinelli turned green.
"We have the information from your boy here plus your twenty grand and new hit list."
"I don't know anything about that, you can't take his word against mine."
"Sit him down at the table, boys."

Mac and Boone grabbed him. The nails were still in the table so they tied his hand down.

"Let's see how tough you are now, Mr. Martinelli," sneered Farichi.

"Now, Mr. Martinelli, who gives you your orders to have Dombrowski do these killings?"

"I don't know anything about any killings," he sneered.

Mac brought the knife down and took off the first joint of his neatly manicured index finger. He stared in disbelief and started to pass out. Farichi gave an evil laugh.

"Wait until he takes off the rest of your fingers, big man." Martinelli turned white.

"I asked you who gave you your orders?" repeated Bronski.

Mac raised the knife.

"Oh, my God, no, please, no, stop, I'll give you the names of my superiors, but it goes higher than them."

"Who are you talking about?"

"There are some bigs in the government involved. Honest, to God. I don't know their names, but they're big."

He gave Bronski the names of four of his superiors.

Farichi laughed. "You're dead, Giovanni."

Bronski took Blake aside.

"This thing is growing like a mushroom. Let's take these guys out to the Army stockade, that will keep them under wraps for awhile."

"Good idea, I'll arrange for some closed vans.

"I think we'd better have a conference with the Chief."

CHAPTER THIRTEEN

An hour later they knocked on Miner's door.
"Come."
He nodded to a couple of chairs when they entered.
Bronski briefed him on what had happened to that point.
"From here on it looks like we're after big game, not only the Mafia, but some government big guns. We're going to need some backing to tackle this."
Miner flipped on the intercom.
"Mona, get me the Vice-president at the White House."
In a few minutes she came back.
"Your party is on the line, Chief."
"Hello, George, how are you?"
"Hello, Frank, I'm fine, and you?"
"Top shape. We need your help, George."
"Name it, Frank."
"I can't discuss it over the phone, I'm sending Bronski and Blake over to talk to you. When would it be convenient?"
"Anytime you say, Frank."
"How about one o'clock this afternoon?"
"I'll be expecting them."
"Thank you, George."
"Anytime, Frank." He broke the connection.
"There you are, boys, get moving."
"Thanks, Chief."

At 12:55 Bronski and Blake drove through the gate at the White House. They showed their ID's and were waved through.
At 12:59 the Vice-president's secretary, Byron, showed them into the office.
"Maj. Bronski and Lt. Col. Blake, Sir."
The Vice-president stood and extended his hand.
"Good afternoon, Gentlemen, have a seat."
"Thank you, Sir. They took the two chairs in front of the desk.

"Now, how can I be of service to you?"

Bronski and Blake explained what had happened.

"My God, I knew a couple of senators had been shot, but I had no idea it had gone this far."

"From here on, Sir, it's a kid glove situation. We've got the names of the Mafia bosses, but to make it stick we'll need Federal warrants. Then it will depend on who the government officials are that have their hands in this."

"Do you think the Mafia bosses will tell you anything?"

Bronski smiled. "We can be pretty persuasive when we have to."

"Alright, let me get you those warrants."

"Since we don't know who the government bigs are, may I suggest that you call someone you know you can trust?"

"I'll get the Chief Justice and have him send blank warrants. You can fill in the names. That should plug any leaks."

"Excellent," said Bronski.

He picked up the phone and dialed a number, spoke to the Chief Justice and told him what he wanted.

"They should be here in about twenty minutes, four blank warrants. My secretary, Byron, will get you coffee or anything else you want while you wait."

They stood. "Thank you very much, Sir, we'll wait in the outer office, we know you are very busy."

"Very well, Byron will let you know when they arrive."

Twenty minutes later a sealed envelope arrived by messenger for the Vice-president. Byron knocked on the door and took it in. When he came out he beckoned to Bronski and Blake.

"Please go in, Gentlemen."

The Vice-president was counter-signing the warrants.

"There you are Gentlemen, this should do the job for you, and good luck."

"Thank you very much, Sir."

"I'd appreciate knowing how you make out and have Frank call me if you need help rounding up the top brass."

"Yes, Sir, we'll see that you get a copy of the final report."

Bronski and Blake checked in with Miner then organized a task force to converge on the Mafia headquarters.

The next morning the estate that housed the Mafia headquarters was surrounded. Telephone line were cut so there would be no communication with the outside. Four men worked their way to the gate and captured the guards before they could spread the alarm.

"Four carloads of armed agents invaded the grounds and surrounded the house.

Bronski, Blake, Mac, and Boone went up to the door. When it opened they pushed their way in. The four men the warrants were for were all at the table in the conference room when Bronski and the others burst through the door.

"Put your hands on the table gentlemen and just sit quiet," said Bronski.

Two men came through the door with gins n their hands.

Mac and Boone swung around.

"Drop your guns boys or these four are dead," snapped Mac.

One of the men at the table gave an order, "Drop them!"

The guns clattered to the floor.

"Now turn around and put your hands on the wall," ordered Boone.

"What's this all about?" asked the man at the table that had given the order.

"We have warrants for you four, Federicci Gennitelli, Francisco Fedderinni, Bruno Galacci, and Gino Pasqualli."

"Ha! Stick your warrants," sneered Gennitelli.

"Not these, they're signed by the Chief Justice and counter-signed by the Vice-president of the United States. Put the cuffs on them Boone."

Boone grinned. "My pleasure." He put the cuffs on the, yanking their arms behind their backs none too gently bringing a yell of pain from all of them, including the two gunmen.

At OSI headquarters they were placed in separate rooms then taken into the interrogating room individually. Gennitelli was taken in first and set at the table.

"Bring Farichi in, Mac," said Bronski. "Now Mr. Gennitelli, I want you to know we have your hit man, Dombrowski, Martinelli, your enforcer, and a few more of your scum bags on ice. We know all about why you are ordering these killings and now we want to know who is behind it all."

"What the hell are you talking about? I ain't saying nothing without my lawyer."

Mac brought Farichi in. When Gennitelli saw his hand wrapped in a bloody bandage, he got nervous.

"What the hell happened to you?"

"They cut off my thumb to make me talk."

"And did you talk?"

"You damn right, I didn't want to lose the rest of my fingers."

"When you get out of here you won't need them."

"Yeah? Let's see how brave your are."

"Martinelli and all your boys have sung us a tune so you might as well join the chorus," said Bronski.

"To hell with you."

"Who give you your orders, Gennitelli?"

He turned and spit on the floor.

"Set him up, boys."

Mac and Boone grabbed him. While Boone held him Mac tied up his hand and then to the table.

"What's going on? What's this for?"

"So you won't run away when the Major starts asking you questions."

"Why should I run away, I ain't answering any questions."

"The Major just asked you one."

"Screw you."

Mac took the first joint of his thumb off.

He looked in astonishment and let loose a stream of four letter words.

"You crazy son-of-a-bitch!" he screamed at Mac.

Mac backhanded him and started his nose bleeding.

"Answer the Major."

"Screw you."

Mac looked at Bronski and shook his head. His knife came down and took off the rest of the thumb. He really screamed then. Farichi laughed an evil laugh. "Now you gonna talk?"

"The Major's waiting," said Mac.

"Fuck you."

Mac took off the first joint of his index finger.

"Oh my God, stop, stop!" he begged.

"OK, talk."

"I can't, they'll kill me," he sobbed.

"Charley, have the boys bring the other three in here."

Charley and the other agent brought in Fedderinni, Galacci, and Pasqualli. When they saw Farichi and Gennitelli with their bloody hands they turned pale.

"I thought you gentlemen would be interested in seeing how we interrogate people like you. Farichi lost a thumb and so far Gennitelli has lost a thumb and an index finger. I asked him who give the orders to wipe out these senators. As yet he hasn't answered me. Of course he has three fingers left on his right hand and five on his left so I'll keep asking. Are you ready, Mr. Gennitelli?"

Silence-----

Mac brought the knife down and took off the first joint of his middle finger. He screamed and started to pass out. Fedderinni turned his head and barfed.

"Perhaps one of you gentlemen would like to take his place for awhile."

Charley grabbed Fedderinni's arm and pulled him towards the table.

He slumped down and pulled back.

"Oh Christ no, I'll tell you."

The others were taken out of the room.

"Bandage Gennitelli and put him on ice," said Bronski.

"They'll kill you if you talk, Francisco," sobbed Gennitelli as they dragged him away.

"To hell with them, I don't want to get mutilated."

"OK, Fedderinni, talk to me, who are the government bigs that are behind this?"

He gave Bronski the names of four senators, three congressmen, and the Attorney General.

"OK, Charley, stuff him away for awhile. We'll take them out to the stockade in a bit."

Charley dragged the sobbing Fedderinni away.

Bronski and Blake knocked on Miner's door.

"Come."

He greeted them as they entered.

"I hope you're bringing me good news."

"Yes and no, Chief."

They showed him the information they had. He read it and emitted a low whistle.

"I think we should show this to the Vice-president." He flipped on the intercom. "Mona, would you get me the Vice-president, please?"

In a few minutes she was back. "Your party is on the line, Chief."

"Hello, George."

"Hello, Frank, what can I do for you?"

"We've got a hot potato, George, and I think you should hear it from Bronski and Blake."

"Send them over, I'll be waiting."

"Thanks, George."

"Anytime, Frank."

The connection was broken.

"Hop to it, boys, he'll be waiting."

Byron opened the door for Bronski and Blake when they arrived.

"Major Bronski and Lt. Col. Blake, are here, Sir." He held the door then closed it after them.

"Come in, Gentlemen." He indicated the chairs in front of his desk.

"Good afternoon, Sir. We thought you should see this. We'll need your help again." Bronski handed him a typewritten sheet of information.

As he read it his eyebrows went up.

"Well I'll be damned!" he exclaimed when he finished. "How do you want to handle this?"

"We'd like a squad of sixteen Marines put at our disposal, four closed vans, and eight warrants. The Marines should be in dressed blues and side arms."

"Where do you want them to meet you?"

"At the Legislature Building."

He picked up his pen and took a sheet of paper out of his desk, then began to write. When he finished he placed the sheet of paper in an envelope, sealed it, then rang for Byron.

"Take this over to the Chief Justice and wait."

After Byron left he picked up the phone and dialed a number.

"Gen. Filmore, please."

"Mr. Vice-president, how can I be of service, Sir?"

"Hello, Robert, how soon can you get me a sixteen man squad, in dress blues, and side arms?"

"Will one hour be soon enough?"

"That will have to do. Call me when they're ready."

"Yes, Mr. Vice-president, the minute they're ready."

"Thank you, Robert." He hung up smiling. "I'll bet he's asking, 'what's that all about?'. They'll be ready in one hour. You did say the Legislature Building? Very well, make yourselves at home in Byron's office and I'll call you as soon as I hear something."

In a little over a half an hour Byron returned and went right into the Vice-president's office. About fifteen minutes later he opened the door and summoned Bronski and Blake to enter.

"Here are your warrants and your Marines will meet you in front of the Legislature Building with the vans. Good luck and, I might add, a fine job."

"Thank you, Sir, and thank you for all your support and help. We'll see that you get a full report."

The Marine squad was lined up in front of the Legislature Building when they got there. Bronski briefed them on what they were to do. He turned to the sergeant in charge of the squad.

"I want you to take this warrant and one man to the federal Building, there pick up the Attorney General. Ask him to accompany you. If he gives you any trouble, show him the warrant. With those signatures he won't give you any argument. Take one of the vans and bring him back here, got that?"

The sergeant grinned and saluted. "Yes, Sir."

"I'll take these three warrants and six men to pick up the congressmen" said Charley.

"Good, the rest of us will go after the senators," said Bronski.

The Senate was in session when Bronski spoke to the guard at the door. He opened it and Bronski led the way to the front of the hall. The room suddenly became quiet.

The Vice-president was in the chairman's seat so Bronski walked up, saluted and handed him a note. He rapped his gavel.

"Will Senators Murphy, Johnson, Peters, and Wilcox please rise."

Bronski motioned to his Marines and two of them went to each senator.

"Will you gentlemen please accompany these Marines?"

The hall became alive with buzzing as the other members began asking each other what was going on. Bronski gave the Vice-president a crisp salute then turned and marched up the aisle followed by the marines and their charges.

In the hall a crowd rushed up to see what was going on. The guards held them back so Bronski could leave.

Outside the congressmen and senators were quickly ushered into the vans and whisked away before the crowd knew what was happening. A couple of reporters and cameramen rushed up, but were quickly collared by the guards.

The vans with their occupants, raced away to the OSI headquarters. Large doors opened and the vans drove inside the building. The eight culprits had been asking what was going on, but the Marines were instructed not to answer any questions.

Inside the building they were taken to the conference room and seated around the table. The Marines stood guard behind them. Bronski and Blake walked to the head of the table and were immediately flooded with demands. Bronski held up his hand for silence.

"Gentlemen, we have in our possession signed statements from four heads of the Mafia naming you eight men as heads of a conspiracy to murder certain senators who were strongly supporting the gun ban bill."

The Attorney General stood up, but was quickly pushed back in his seat by two Marines.

"See here, I am the Attorney General of the United States, how dare you accuse me of such a thing?"

"We know who you are Mr. Attorney General, and rest assured that you would not be here if we did not have concrete proof of your involvement. You are all to be taken to the Army stockade at Fort Clark and held there until you are brought to trial for your crimes. You will be held without bail, but you may give us the names of your attorneys and we will contact them for you."

"You can't do this, it's illegal," cried Wilcox.

"So is murdering senators, Mr. Wilcox."

Handcuffs and waist chains were brought in and over screaming protests the prisoners were secured.

Back in the vans they were transported to the Fort Clark stockade, with the exception of Senator Peters whom Bronski and Blake recognized as the weak link in the chain.

After the others had been taken away, Bronski and Blake took Peters down to the interrogating room where they met Mac and Pat.

"Bring Farichi in, boys."

"Yes, Sir, Major."

"Sit down, Senator."

Peters sat nervously at the table.

Farichi came in with the sergeants, holding his hand in a sling.

"This is Mr. Farichi, Senator, he's a Mafia soldier. We had to use a little persuasion to loosen up his tongue, but he told us what we wanted to know."

"They cut off your fucking fingers if you don't talk, they're crazy."

Peters turned pale.

"OK, boys, take Farichi back to his room," said Bronski.

"Now, Senator, we have most of the facts and most of the guilty parties, so why don't you tell us who is putting up the money to stop the gun ban bill?"

Peters broke down and with his head in his arms on the table began to sob without control. It took almost thirty minutes for him to regain control of himself before he could talk. Bronski and Blake stood by waiting patiently.

He finally calmed down and gave them the names of three millionaires who had big interest in the weapons industry.

"Thank you, Senator." He turned to Mac and Boone. "Let's get the rest of the scum bags in there ready to take to the stockade. The two Marines out there will give you a hand."

"I'll call for a couple of closed vans," said Charley.

"CHAPTER FIFTEEN"

Later in Col. Miner's office, Bronski and Blake laid out the final phase of the investigation for him.

"I think we'd better let the Vice-president make the decision on this one, too, this could make for a very delicate situation." He called Mona on the intercom. "Mona, would you get me the Vice-president, please?"

In a few minutes she called back.

"He's not available at the moment, Chief, but Byron is getting your message to him."

A few minutes later she called back again.

"Your party is on the line, Chief."

"Hello, George."

"Hello, Frank. Your boys really stirred the bees, you wouldn't believe the rumors that are flying around, but of course no one knows anything. I just came from the President and he's furious, he's ready to have a hanging party without a trial. Now, what can I do for you, Frank?"

"Bronski and Blake have the final link in the chain, but I think you should make the decision on this one."

"Very well, send them over."

When Bronski and Blake finished giving the Vice-president the names of the three men behind the conspiracy, he sat there shaking his head.

"This will have to be handled very discretely, if word of this got out it could cause a financial crisis. I think I have a plan. We'll have to move fast. I'm going to invite these three to dinner tonight. The invitation will be such that they won't be able to refuse. You both will be there. At the finish of dinner, I'll say that you have something interesting to say. You can explain what it's about in case they should ask. You can have a Marine escort there to take them away. Do you both have a tux?"

"Yes, Sir, we have our mess dress uniforms."

"Fine, wear them and I'll see you at seven p.m."

At eight o'clock, after cocktails, Bronski and Blake, in their mess dress uniforms, were enjoying a fine dinner at the Vice-president's mansion. Their quarries were very talkative and full of questions about the military.

Bronski and Blake answered their questions as best they could. As the brandy was being served, the Vice-president announced, "Gentlemen, Major Bronski has something very interesting to tell you."

Briefly Bronski told them about the murder of the senators, Senator Egan's golf partner, who was killed by mistake, and the shooting of the two speakers at the rally. He covered the capture of Dombrowski, explained the involvement of the Mafia and their eventual capture. Then he told them about the part the senators, congressmen, and the Attorney General played, and how they were taken into custody.

The three men began to stir in their seats.

"And now, Gentlemen, we come to the conclusion. Every chain has its weak link and in this case the chain broke. One of the senators gave us the names of the three men behind this entire conspiracy."

At a signal from Bronski, four Marines came into the room and stood behind the three men.

"As soon as you three men finish your brandy, these four impressive looking Marines will escort you to your new quarters."

The three men looked at each other.

"Mr. Vice-president may we use your study for a short conference?"

The Vice-president raised his hand and signaled the butler.

"Right this way, gentlemen," He opened the study door.

The door closed behind them and there was a silence for several long minutes. Suddenly three shots rang out in the study.

Bronski, Blake, and the four Marines started for the door. The Vice-president held up his hand. "No need to rush, Gentlemen, I think they just carried out their own sentences and saved the government the trouble and expense of a long drawn out trial."

The open door revealed the bodies of the three men. A small caliber automatic lay on the floor beside them.

"Just as well," said the Vice-president, "this would have ruined them. Now to see that the others are properly punished. This country owes you boys a debt of gratitude. Of course none of you know what happened here tonight." The four Marines smiled.

When Bronski and Blake were ready to leave, the Vice-president shook their hands.

"Thank God this country has men like you to bring these guilty parties to justice."

Back in the office the next morning, Bronski flipped on the intercom switch.

"Mona, can you come in here for a minute?"

The door opened and she stuck her head in. "What is it, love?"

"Mona, you know the editor of the New York Herald pretty well, don't you?"

"Yes, Clint Baxter is and old friend of the family."

"I wonder if you could get him to do me a favor?"

"Depends on what kind of a favor, but we can go talk to him about it."

"Why don't you give him a call and see if you can set up an appointment for this morning and then maybe take him to lunch afterwards."

"I'll try." She picked up the phone and dialed a number.

"New York Herald, Mr. Baxter's office."

"Hello, Evelyn, Mona Ferguson, is Clint in?"

"Yes, Mona, I'll connect you."

"Hello, Mona, to what do I owe this honor?"

"Hello, Clint. Can we have an appointment with you this morning and then take you to lunch?"

"I never refuse a bribe, especially from a beautiful lady, come on over."

"Fine, we'll be there in about an hour."

"OK, who's we?"

"Joe Bronski and me."

"See you in an hour."

At 1100 hours they knocked on Clint Baxter's door.

"Come in, come in."

"Hello, Clint, you remember Joe Bronski."

"Hello, Mona darling. How are you, Joe?"

"Fine, Sir, thank you for seeing us."

"Not at all. What can I do for you?"

"I think I have a hot story for you and I need a favor."

"I'll do what I can, what's it about?"

Bronski laid out the entire stoty for him.

"Wow! How much of this can I print?"

"All of it now that we have the guilty parties in custody. What I want to do is release all the Mafia boys and then have you print a story saying they all talked and revealed Mafia secrets to us and we're planning to come down on them."

"You know what will happen to them, don't you?"

"Yes, I figure, let them take care of their own."

"You have a deal. Can I put one of my boys on it to get the rest of the story?"

"Yes, I'll give him all the help I can."

"Good, now let's go to lunch, but you're to be MY guests."

Bronski knocked on Col. Miner's door.

"Come."

"Hello, Chief, have you got a few minutes?"

"Of course, what's on your mind?"

Bronski laid out is plan.

"You know, I think I need a hearing aid. I haven't heard a word you said except that you were going to release the Mafia boys from the stockade for lack of evidence."

Bronski smiled. "That's Right, Chief. Now I have to go see about their release from the Fort stockade."

Thirty minutes later Bronski was facing the Mafia men.

"We're releasing you on your own recognizance. I've ordered limousines to return you to your headquarters."

"Smart punk Major," sneered Gennitelli, "you didn't think you could hold us, did you? You ain't heard the last of us."

"I'm sorry for the inconvenience, Mr. Gennitelli, you take care of that hand."

In the limousine Gennitelli bragged. "He got a little smarts, you see he calls me MISTER Gennitelli. He even sends chauffeurs for us."

124

As they pulled away Bronski laughed and called out, "Don't forget to pay for the limousines, Mr. Gennitelli!" He turned to Blake. "Remind me to pick up the evening edition of the Herald, I understand there's suppose to be an interesting story in it."

Blake laughed. "I'll have Mona pick up several copies for the office."

Bronski, Blake, and Mona sat in Bronski's office looking over the evening edition of the New York Herald.

"Quite a story," said Mona, "Clint was really pleased to get it from you."

"Well, he can release all the facts not that it's over. I'll be interested to see what the morning edition has to say."

Mona and Blake smiled.

There was a meeting at the Mafia headquarters late that evening. The Godfather sat at the head of the table with the evening edition of the Herald in front of him. Twelve heads of the organization were seated around the table, including Signores Gennitelli, Fedderinni, Galacci, and Pasqualli.

The Godfather looked up from the paper.

"What happened to your hand Feddericci?" he asked.

"That son-of-a-bitch of a Major had his man cut off my fingers to make me talk."

"So, did you talk?"

"No, Godfather, I would never talk."

"That is not what the paper says and they would no say that you did if your didn't."

"I swear I didn't."

"But you let yourself get in a position where you could be questioned, all four of you, and the others. Now you put us in an awkward position." He shook his head. "And what is this bill for three limousines?"

"That punk Major was suppose to pay for them."

"It looks like he stuck us for it." He shook his head again.

"You four leave the room, we must make a decision."

Outside Gennitelli bragged. "Smart punk Major, thinks they'll take his word against mine, you will see."

Bronski walked into the office with the morning edition of the Herald. He looked for Mona, but she wasn't at her desk. In a moment she came in with a tray on which was a pot of coffee and three cups.

"Hi, Joe," Charley greeted him. "We should have kept those boys in custody and this wouldn't have happened."

He held up the front page of the paper showing the headline. It read,

"NINE BULLET RIDDLED BODIES FOUND IN THE CITY DUMP. BELIEVED TO BE MEMBERS OF THE MAFIA"

Beneath that the story read;

"Nine bullet riddled bodies were found by workmen when

they reported for work at the city dump this morning early. It appeared that this was the work of the Mafia and was the results of the story that appeared in this paper last evening. Four of he bodies were identified as heads of he Mafia, Federicci Genitelli, Francisco Fedderinni, Bruno Galacci, and Gino Pasqualli. Giovanni Martinelli, know as the "Enforcer" for the Mafia, was also among the bodies. The police were puzzled over the fact that some of the bodies were missing fingers. They appeared to have been chopped off.

"That must be the method used by the Mafia to make them reveal how much they talked," commissioner Murphy was quoted as saying, "those Eyetalians can be pretty brutal."

"You're right, Charley, I was afraid something like this would happen if we let them go. Perhaps we shouldn't have told that reporter that they revealed Mafia secrets to us," said Bronski, turning his head to hide a smile.

On the same front page another news item read: "THE BODIES OF THREE OF NEW YORK'S MILLIONAIRES WERE RECOVERED AFTER THEIR YACHT CAPSIZED OFF CAPE COD DURING LAST NIGHT'S STORM."

Bronski shook his head and looked serious. "Too bad about those three millionaires, isn't it? I guess money doesn't mean anything when you number comes up."

"CHAPTER EIGHTEEN"

Bronski knocked on Col. Miner's door.

"Come."

"Here you are, Chief, all wrapped up in a neat bundle, complete except for a pink ribbon." He laid the folder on Miner's desk.

"Good work, Joe. Here's one for you." He handed him an official looking envelope. Bronski opened it and read the contents. He smiled.

"VERY GOOD! Thank you, Chief." It was his promotion to Lt. Colonel.

"You certainly deserve it, Joe. Here, these are my old silver leaves, I'd be proud if you'd wear them. This came by special messenger." He handed Bronski a letter. It read:

> To: Frank J. Miner
> From: The Joint Chiefs of Staff
> Congratulations: Your promotion to the rank of Brigadier General has been approved by the Congressional Military Affairs Committee for Promotions.
> Signed

John R. Fairwell, Major General

"Frank, congratulations, let me be the first to congratulate you, General," said Bronski, grinning from ear to ear.

The folder labeled "OPERATION SHARP SHOOTER" lay open on Frank Miner's desk. Bronski's complete report was contained therein. He smiled when he read the title.

The final report read:

The murder of the aforementioned victims has been solved and the murderer taken into custody, along with all the persons involved in the conspiracy to kill the gun ban bill. All parties have been brought to trial, found guilty, and proper punishment is being meted out.

Members of the Mafia who were to be brought to trial for their involvement have been eliminated, presumably by members of their own organization.

Complete details re enclosed.

All agent of the Office of Special Investigations should be commended for their participation in solving this case.

End of report,
Signed,

Joseph Bronski, Major
Office of Special Investigations
United States Army

JB:mf

Copies to :
The President of the United States
The Vice-president of the United States
The Acting Attorney General

Later that evening, Brig/Gen. Frank Miner, Lt. Col. Charley Blake, Lt. Col. Joe Bronski, and Mona Ferguson were enjoying cocktails and dinner in Mona's apartment to celebrate the promotions of Miner and Bronski.

"It couldn't be more deserved," said Charley, holding up his glass, "to two of the best."

"Hear! Hear!" They all lifted up their glasses and drank a toast to Brig/Gen. Miner and Lt. Col. Bronski.

Bronski lowered his head and turned away for a minute to hide the moisture in his eyes, appreciating the fact that these were not only his colleagues, but good and close friends.

PART THREE

"Operation Find A Gun"

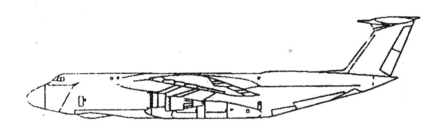

c5a

"OPERATION FIND A GUN"

Mona Ferguson removed her coat, carefully hung it in the closet, and sat down at her desk to check her messages from the night operator. The phone rang.

"Good morning, Office of Special Investigations."

"Good morning, this is Capt. Fitch, aide to Gen. Harris, Commander of Fort Rycker. Is Lt. Col. Bronski in?"

"No, he isn't yet, can I take a message?"

"Yes, would you tell him to call Gen. Harris the minute he gets in and tell him it's urgent?"

"Yes, I will, I have the number."

"Thank you." The connection was broken.

Ten minutes later Lt. Col. Bronski walked in.

"Good morning, my sweet, how are you this lovely day?"

"Good morning, love, but I'm not sure what kind of a day it's going to be for you. Capt. Fitch called, Gen. Harris wants to talk to you right away. I'll put through the call for you."

"Thanks, Mona."

She dialed the number and the phone rang once when Capt. Fitch picked it up. "Good morning, Gen. Harris' office Capt. Fitch speaking."

"Hello, Captain, I have Col. Bronski for you."

"Thank you, I'll connect you with the General."

"Gen. Harris here."

"This is Col. Bronski, Sir."

"Hello, Joe, Jesus Christ, someone is stealing our weapons and ammunition."

"You're kidding me, General, what's missing?"

"I just got a call from Gen. Hoyt. He said that four of our fifty cal. machine guns and two seventy-five mm field pieces are missing. He's checking the ammunition to see how much is missing."

"What the hell, Sir, is someone going to start a revolution?"

"Damned if I know. How soon can you get down here?"

"I can be there at about 1100 hours."

"Good, I'll have Hart meet you at the air strip. He'll be

available if you want him to work with you on this. You two made a good team the last time."

"Thank you, Sir, I'll check with you when I get there."

"Good, Joe, and thank you for coming."

"Is the Chief in yet, Mona?"

"Yes, he came in while you were talking to Gen. Harris."

"Good, meet me in his office."

Bronski knocked three times on Gen. Miner's door.

"Come."

Bronski held the door for Mona and they both walked in.

Miner looked up from his desk. "What the hell are you two looking so serious about?"

"Good morning, Chief. I just talked to Gen. Harris at Fort Rycker. He said someone is stealing his weapons and ammunition. He wants me to come down there right away."

"Somebody going to start a gang war?"

"Sounds bigger than that, Chief. He says they're missing four 50 cal. machine guns and two 75mm field pieces. They're checking to see how much ammunition is missing."

"Holy cow, when are you leaving?"

"I'll be leaving soon as I can check my desk and get out of here. I wanted Mona to hear this. She'll probably be running down some information for me and I wanted to clue you in on it."

"Thanks, Joe, and if you need anything, holler."

"Right, Chief, I'll talk to you later. Come on, Mona."

"I'll call you as soon as I know what's happening and give you a number where you can reach me at night."

"OK, Joe, please be careful."

At 1058 hours, Bronski greased the 310 onto the runway at Fort Rycker air strip. The "Follow Me" jeep swung out on the runway to lead him to the parking tarmac.

He swung the twin engine aircraft into the tie down spot and cut the engine at the ground crewman's signal.

After doing his post flight check he stepped out on the wing , climbed down and took Gen. Hart's outstretched hand.

"Hello, Joe, good to see you."

"Hello, Bret, looks like we've got another one, huh?"

"Yes, only this time they're not blowing up generals, but they're sure going to blow something to hell. How's Mona?"

"Why don't you come up and check on her yourself once in awhile? I'm sure she'd like that."

Bret laughed. "Maybe I'll just deliver all your messages personally and save you the trouble of phoning."

Bronski laughed. "I think you're serious. OK, tell me what's happening."

"Gen. Hoyt, head of ordnance, called this morning all excited about missing machine guns and field pieces. He check again after you talked to the Old Man and found that there were 400 rounds of seventy-fives and 2000 rounds of fifties missing. He's about to have a tizzy."

"When did they first miss all this?"

"This morning. It seems one of the sergeants was walking through the depot and noticed empty spaces where the field pieces were suppose to be. Then he looked around and found some of the fifties were missing. They're looking around now to see what else has been misplaced. I'm being facetious."

They walked to the car. Corporal Lind greeted him.

"Hello, Colonel, good to see you again, too bad it's always when we got trouble."

"Hello, Corporal, good to see you. I guess we don't have to check for bombs this time, do we?"

Lind laughed. "I hope not, Sir. Besides somebody would have stolen them by now."

Hart laughed. "Bad joke, Lind, take us to headquarters." Bronski and Lind joined in the laugh.

Captain Fitch saluted as Bronski and Hart walked in.

"I'm sure glad to see you, Colonel, Gen. Harris is fit to be tied. I'll announce you."

He opened the door to the General's office. "Gen. Hart and Col. Bronski are here, Sir."

"Come in, Gentlemen."

Gen. Harris stood up and offered his hand to Bronski.

"Thanks for coming, Joe, looks like we have another bummer on our hands. I don't know how anyone could have gotten those pieces out of the camp without someone seeing them."

"Have you checked the guards?"

"No, I'll leave that up to you." The intercom light flashed on. "Yes, Fitch?"

"Sir, Gen. Minten from Fort Johns is on the line."

"Excuse me, Gentlemen." "Hello, Henry, how are you?"

"Hello, George, I'm not sure. Are you missing any ordnance?"

"Yes, don't tell me you are, too?"

"Yes, some machine guns, field pieces, and a rocket launcher."

"What the hell is going on? I've got Col. Bronski from the OSI sitting right here. I called this morning and got him to come down to investigate."

"Good, let me talk to him."

He handed the phone to Bronski. "Gen. Minten from Fort Johns."

"Hello, General, how can I help you?"

"Hello, Colonel, It looks like we've got an epidemic of ordnance thefts. When you're through there would you come here and see what you can find out?"

"Yes, Sir. I don't know how long it's going to take me here, but I'll call you when I'm ready to leave."

"Very good, I'll wait for your call." He hung up.

"This looks to me like it's all tied together. I wonder if any of the other bases have lost anything?"

"While you're checking here, I'll have Fitch check around."

"I wonder who would want all that stuff and why? I'd better do some fast checking. We'll get back to you, Sir," said Bronski and he stood up. Hart followed.

Gen. Harris stood up and extended his hand. "Glad to have you on the job, Joe, good luck to you both. I assume that you'd like to have Gen. Hart work with you on this?"

"I'd sure appreciate it, Sir."

"You got him."

"Well, Bret, here we go again. Let's go over to Ordnance and see what we can dig up."

Bronski had Gen. Hoyt call in everybody who worked in the Ordnance Depot or had access to it. One by one they questioned those available. Bronski took down all the conversation in shorthand. He wanted to know where each one had been in the past several days and what time, also who they had been with.

He checked the size and weight of the ammunition containers and crates. He wanted to know when they had last been seen and by whom. The nearest he could figure out, it had all been disappearing gradually over the past month.

"How come this hadn't been reported sooner if pieces have been disappearing over that long a period?" he asked the sergeant in charge of the warehouse.

"I'm sorry, Sir, but we only take a quick inventory every two months. It was by accident that I noticed the empty spaces yesterday."

"Might be a good idea to take an inventory more often." he suggested. "Let's go check the gate guards and see if their logs can tell us what trucks have gone off the base in the past month," said Bronski.

"Good idea. We might also check the motor pool and see what vehicles have been checked out, trucks I mean," suggested Hart.

"While we're at it we might as well check out the gate guards and see where they have been in the past several weeks."

"Those pieces could have been disassembled and small

pieces gone out in cars and pickups. The larger parts would have to have gone out in a truck," said Hart.

"Do you have a couple of men you can trust to check up on these stories we've been getting? It'll save us a lot of time and work."

"Yes, I have just the men for it. I'll take care of it just as soon as we get finished at the gate."

"Alright, while you're doing that I'll call the office and have Mona do some checking to see who might be wanting this stuff and why."

Hart grinned. "Want me to go ask her personally?"

Bronski laughed. "You're too eager, it would take you too long."

They went over the logs of the gate guards and found that every truck that went out was checked off as legal.

"What d'you mean when you say legal?" asked Bronski.

"We check the bills and see if the load agrees."

"Do you check the crates and boxes to see what they contain?"

"Sir, we can't open every crate and box that goes out of here."

"That's exactly what you're suppose to do, mister. Right now they're missing four machine guns, two field pieces, and some ammunition. That certainly wasn't hauled out of here without being crated. Can you tell from your logs which trucks had crates or boxes?"

"Some of them went out after I went off duty. You'd have to check with the guards on the other shifts."

"We'd better have the General issue an order that every box or crate that goes out of here will have to opened for inspection," said Bronski.

"As Chief of Staff I have the authority to issue that order. Here, give me your log and I'll attach a note to it right now," said Hart.

"I'm going to call in a couple more agents to track down those crates and boxes to see where they went and who received them. Where would anybody get enough lumber to crate this stuff?" asked Bronski.

"From our carpenter shop," said Hart.

"After we make these calls, let's check that out"

The sergeant in charge of the carpenter shop discovered that he was missing quite a lot of crating lumber and was just making out a report when Bronski and Hart walked in.

"Looks like someone is building a honeymoon cabin, Sir."

Bronski smiled. "No, Sergeant," he explained what happened.

"Hell, Sir, that explains it, there's enough missing to do the job."

They went back to Ordnance to finish questioning the rest of the men.

"You guys had better be telling the truth because we're going to check all of your stories. We aren't here to reveal who you're sleeping with, if you're innocent this will be to your advantage."

When they were finished questioning, Bronski asked Hart, "Did some of those guys seem a little evasive to you?"

"Yes, I made a note of those I thought might be hiding something so we could discuss it later. Here's the list of the ones that I noted."

Bronski checked his shorthand notes.

"These are the same ones that I wondered about. We'd better check them out pretty thoroughly. I'll call the office and get a couple more men down here to work on that."

Bronski picked up the phone and dialed the office.

"Good afternoon, OSI."

Hello, Mona, Joe here."

"Hello, Joe, are you doing any good?"

"Just asking a few questions right now. We need some more help. Are Gutterman, Walls, and Benson around?"

"Gutterman and Benson are here, but Walls is out in the field. Nelson is here."

"Good, call them and see if they're available."

"Hold on, they're in the conference room having coffee, I'll call them" She called the conference room and got back to Bronski. "They're available, Joe, and want to know how soon you want them?"

"Tell them to get down here a.s.a.p and plan to stay for several days."

"OK, Joe, I'll get them on their way."

"Thanks, honey, and by the way there's a young handsome General standing here chomping at the bit. He wants to deliver these messages personally."

"Mona laughed. "Give Bret my love, and I'll talk to you later."

"OK, will do." He turned to Bret. "Mona sends her love. I've got three men coming, Gutterman, Benson, and Nelson. You haven't met Howie Nelson, good man. They can check out these alibis for us. They'll be here this evening. In the meantime we can do some more snooping. I think we should fly over to Fort Johns in the morning and check with Gen. Minten."

"CHAPTER TWO"

At 2000 hours they took two cars to the air strip to pick up the three agents.

"I sure like the looks of that 310 you fly. It looks like it's going like hell even when it's sitting on the ground."

"Yes, with those 300 hp engines it moves right along and performs like a champ. Who flies that old Beaver?"

"Col. Rodriguez from Artillery. He goes over to west Texas once in awhile. Says to see his family, but I think he has a honey over there."

"I should think he would fly something beside that old DeHavalin work horse."

"For some reason he likes it."

A Beech Baron circled the field and turned on final approach to the runway. "There's our boys now. Looks like Nelson at the controls."

"How can you tell?"

"By the way he made his approach. Most high time pilots develop their own style. If you know them you recognize it."

The "Follow Me" jeep met the Baron after he touched down lightly and turned off the runway, then guided him to the parking tarmac.

The plane swung into the tiedown spot and the ground crewman signaled to cut the engines. His crew chocked the wheels and tied it down. In a few minutes the three men emerged.

Bronski greeted them. "You know these two, Bret, and this is Major Howie Nelson. Howie, Gen. Bret Hart."

They shook hands then Hart turned to the other two.

"You in trouble again, Bret?" asked Gutterman.

"No, Joe just like to come down here and mingle with us real soldiers."

"Ouch! Sorry I asked," he said laughing.

"Good to see you," laughed Bret as they shook hands.

"Have you eaten yet?"

"No, Mona rushed us out before we had a chance to get anything."

"Let's go over to the "O Club", we can brief you while we eat."

Hart had the mess officer give them a table in a secluded corner so they could talk. It was near the end of the dinner hour so there were only a few people in the dining room.

"Here's what happened and what we have done so far," said Bronski.

Bronski and Hart filled them in on the details. "What we would like two of you to do is check up on the shipment of crates and boxes that went out of here in the past month. Here's a list of trucks and their bills of lading. We want to know where they went and who received them. If you can, see if the contents agree with what's listed on the bills.

"The other one we'd like to have check on the stories given us by the men that work in Ordnance. I don't have to tell you to be thorough, Bret has a couple of men working on it, you can work with them. The same thing has happened over at Fort Johns. Bret and I are flying over there in the morning to check with Gen. Minten."

"I'll work on the alibis. What if we run into some discrepancies in their stories?" asked Nelson.

"Take the guilty parties into custody and try to get the truth out of them," said Bronski.

"If you run into any delicate situations where it might be advisable to enlist the help of a female, I have a master sergeant in my office who is sharp as a tack. You can get her to assist you. Her name is Carol Man. I'll alert her that you may be needing her help," said Hart.

At his office Hart introduced Bronski to Carol. "This is Lt. Col. Joe Bronski, Carol, one of the top investigators for the OSI. We're working together on this missing ordnance thing. There will be another investigator checking on the stories the men in Ordnance gave us. He and our men may need your help. That will be Major Nelson."

"I'm pleased to meet you, Colonel. I've heard a lot about

141

you. Don't worry, I'll take good care of your major."

"I'm pleased to meet you, Carol," said Bronski, all the while holding her hand and smiling.

Hart smiled. "I guess that makes us even, Joe. I'll explain later, Carol," he said as she gave him a funny look. "You can let go of her hand now, Joe."

Bronski blushed. Carol smiled and winked at him.

When Bronski and Hart arrived at the air strip, Bronski noticed the Beaver gone. He smiled. "Looks like the Colonel is off visiting his lady love again."

"He's been doing that a lot lately, he must be in heat."

Their flight to Fort Johns was a short one. Gen. Minten and his Chief of Staff, Col. Karathers, met them at the air strip.

"I'm glad to see you, Colonel, and you Gen. Hart. I've had calls from Fort Lewis and Fort MacKenzie and they both have the same problem."

"I think I'd best get to a phone, General," said Bronski.

"We'll go to my office."

Bronski dialed his office number.

Mona answered. "Good morning, OSI."

"Hello, Mona, Joe. Is Charley in?"

"Yes, Joe. You sound upset, is something wrong?"

"Yes, Mona, get Charley and stay on the line."

"What's up, Joe?"

"This thing is growing like a weed, Charley. Bret and I are at Fort Johns. Gen. Minten just told us that Fort Lewis and Fort MacKenzie are missing weapons. Bret and I can't possibly handle all of this so can you go to Fort Lewis and MacKenzie and start the investigation there? Take plenty of men with you. I asked Mona to stay on the line so she'll know what's going on."

"I'm here, Joe."

"Fine, here's what we found out and did at Rycker." Bronski briefed Blake.

"I'll keep Mona informed about what's going on here. Again, take plenty of help."

"OK, Joe, I'll be out of here in about an hour."

Bronski turned to Gen. Minten. "That was Col. Blake, we work together. He'll start the investigation at Lewis and MacKenzie while we go to work here."

"You seem to have a pretty close relationship."

"Maybe you don't approve of addressing fellow officers by their first names. It's easier when we're working together than using military courtesy. How we do our job is more important than our rank."

"I can understand that," said Gen. Minten.

"Can you put a car and driver at our disposal, Sir?"

"Of course." He picked up the phone and dialed the motor pool. "Send a car and driver over to headquarters for Gen. Hart and Col. Bronski." He hung up. "It will be a few minutes. If there is anything else you need, just let Col. Karathers know and please keep me posted."

The car pulled up as they came out. "Take us to the Ordnance Depot, driver, and what's your name, Corporal?"

"Yes, Sir, and it's Tate, Sir, Josh Tate."

"OK, Josh, we'll probably be quite awhile in Ordnance so just hang loose."

"Yes, Sir, I'll be waiting."

"If you want to go have a cup of coffee or something, go ahead, you'll have plenty of time."

He grinned. "Yes, Sir."

Col. Sorensen was in charge of the Ordnance Depot. They found him in his office when they walked in. He rose when they entered.

"Good morning, I'm Col. Sorenson. What can I do for you, Gentlemen?'

"Good morning, this is Gen. Hart and I'm Col. Bronski. We're here to investigate the missing ordnance. Can you give us a list of the missing pieces?"

"Yes, I have the list right here. We took inventory as soon as we discovered the pieces missing."

Bronski read off the list.

"Four 50 cal. machine guns, one 75 mm field piece, four 60 mm mortars, one rocket launcher. Hmmmmm," he mused.

143

"Doesn't a rocket launcher have to be mounted on a half track or something to carry it?"

"Yes, the whole thing is missing, we just listed it as one unit."

"How could anyone get that out the gate without being seen?" asked Hart.

"Actually all this disappeared when we were out on maneuvers, it never came back from the field."

"When did you come back?"

"The day before yesterday."

"Ouch, it's going to be a bear to track this stuff now, there will be no record of it going out the gate," said Hart. "We'll need the names of the crewmen on these pieces."

"I can furnish you with that information."

"We'll also need a roster of all the men under you," said Bronski, "and a list of everyone with access to the depot."

A corporal knocked on the door and came in. He handed Sorenson a message.

"Well, this will help you, the crew on the launcher is AWOL. I'll get the men lined up so you can question them."

"I'm going to call the office and get as many men as I can down here to search for that rocket launcher and its crew. A thing like that should be pretty hard to hide," said Bronski.

"You go ahead. In the meantime I'll start doing some questioning," said Hart.

Hart and Sorenson went out, Bronski reached for the phone. ———

"Hi, Mona, Joe here."

"Hi, love, what's up?"

"Get Frank and stay on the line."

"Hello, Joe, what can I do for you?"

"I'll need as many men as I can get, Chief, we have some high power searching to do. Among other weapons, they're missing a rocket launcher, half track and all."

"I'll get right on it, Joe, and get back. Where are you now?"

"Fort Johns. Mona has the number and she knows where to send them. I'll call back tonight and give you a full report." He hung up.

"You know who to call, Mona, and I'll make a few calls myself."

"Right, Chief, done."

Gen. Frank Miner, head of the Office of Special Investigations, dialed a number.

"51st Air Recon, Sgt. Lane."

"This is Gen. Miner, Sergeant, is Gen. Nickeslen in?"

"Yes sir, General, I'll connect you."

"Hello, Frank, how've you been?"

"Fine, Wayne, and you?"

"Top shape, what's on your mind?"

"The Army's got a problem, someone is stealing their weapons. I've got Bronski, Blake, and every available man on it."

"How can I help, Frank?"

"Bronski is at Fort Johns. They're missing, among other things, a rocket launcher, carrier and all. I'm sending every available man for the search. The reason I'm calling you is that they may need some assistance from your stick jockeys and an L19 to do some air searching. That thing should be hard to hide and I thought some of that new infrared equipment you have might do the trick. I don't know if Joe will need you, but I thought I'd put you on alert just in case."

"I'll put a couple of crews on stand by, Frank. But ours are O1's not L19's. Tell Joe to call me if he needs us."

"Thanks, Wayne, I'll give him the word. What's the difference between an O1 and an L19?"

Gen. Nickelsen laughed. "Not a single thing except the serial numbers, and the markings."

"Oh," laughed Frank, "just send us one of those bird dogs."

"Anytime, Frank, talk to you later."

"Mona when you get a chance call and leave word for Joe that Gen. Nickelsen has a couple of crews with bird dogs standing by in case he needs them."

"OK, Chief, I have sixteen men on the way and should be there in about three hours."

"Good work, Mona."

Four planes landed at Fort Johns air strip. Bronski and Hart met them with five cars. "Hi, men, this is Gen. Bret Hart, he's working with us on this thing." He briefed them. "We'll look for that launcher, that should be the hardest to hide. We'll start where they were having their maneuvers. The Air Force is standing by to give us some assistance with a couple of search crews in case we need them. You drivers, we'll send a car from the motor pool to pick you up so you won't have to walk back. I'm sorry, I should have ordered an extra car."

They smiled. "No sweat, Sir," said one of the drivers.

Bronski and Hart with sixteen men spread out to search the area where the maneuvers had been held.

They had been searching in pairs for about three hours, when from the edge of the wooded area, one of the pairs called for Bronski and Hart. When they got there, the men pointed to a large clump of bushes where body parts were exposed.

An examination showed that the four victims all had their throats cut. They were dressed in jungle fatigues.

"Bret, why don't you get on the radio and have Sorenson come out to identify and remove the remains? I'll bet they're the crew from the launcher," said Bronski. "Let's search the perimeter and see if we can determine which way they drove that thing, there's bound to be some tracks of some kind."

One of the pairs signaled they found something. The tracks from the half track were plainly visible and another set of tracks from a semi-tractor and low boy trailer were also visible.

"Looks like they loaded it on a low boy trailer and hauled it away," said Bronski, "now the question is, which way did they go?"

"Let's follow the tracks and see where they lead us," suggested Hart.

"Bret, I'd like you to stay here and show Sorenson where the bodies are and find out if any other men are missing, you can catch up to us when you're finished."

The tracks lead them to a black top road so they followed that for about ten miles until they came to a dirt road that turned off to the right. They stopped to examine it.

"Here's their tracks, let's follow them and see where they go."

Two miles or so down the road they came to a small clearing.

"Look at all those scraps of lumber, Joe."

"Let's take a look."

"Looks like they stopped and built something. I wonder if they built a box around that thing to hide it? The tracks keep going so let's see where they take us."

They followed the dirt road until it forked. The tracks took the left fork. Following this they came back to the black top. Turning back on this it finally took them to where it dead ended at a highway going east and west.

"Well, we've got two choices, we can go east or west."

One of the men got out and was inspecting the road for tracks.

"Look here, Joe!" he called, "they turned west, see the tracks on the dirt shoulder where where they had to make a sharp turn. It must be a long trailer with a jeep on the rear to take the load."

"A jeep?"

"Yeah, it's a rig with four extra sets of wheels they hook on the rear to help distribute the weight. That's why when they cut the corner the wheels went off the road onto the shoulder. Nice of them to leave a trail for us."

"Makes sense, let's follow the highway and question any businesses and people in houses along the way, maybe someone saw something. First phone I get to I'll call the Highway Patrol and see if any of their cruisers have seen anything and put them on alert. It would sure help if we knew what color that rig was. I'll call the Air Force and have them put one of their crews in the air for us."

147

They stopped at the first gas station they came to. Joe went to the phone. One of the men got out to question the young attendant.

"Did you happen to notice a semi with a low boy trailer and a heavy load, possibly a big box, go by here in the past couple of days?"

"Yeah, two three days ago, had a big box on the trailer, looked like a shack or something, I wondered what it was. The rig was olive drab, you now, Army color. Had some other crates stacked on it, too. There was a jeep in front of it with a couple of guys in fatigues, you know, like a pilot car, had an amber light on top."

"Thanks son, you've been a big help." He went to Bronski.

"We know what we're looking for now, Joe." He repeated what the attendant told him.

"That figures, I wonder where they're taking the stuff? They'd be turning south if they were going to ship it out of the country. A couple of you come with me and the rest of you keep tracking that thing. I'll get the Highway Patrol alerted, then call the Air Force and brief them on the target. They should be able to spot it from the air with no trouble if it's still on the road. They'll be in a couple of O1's, you know, they're the same as our L19's, so you'll know what they look like. When you spot them, give them a call on 122.9, so they can pin point you."

Just as Bronski and his men were turning back on the highway, Hart pulled up alongside. He hailed Bronski and said he had some information for him.

"Sorenson came out and identified the bodies. They were the launcher crew. They were getting pretty ripe, made one of his men sick. He said there was also four others AWOL. He's put out an APB on them to all law enforcement people."

"That must be the crew that has the launcher and the semi. We know which way they're heading. They've tried to hide the launcher by building a box around it. Some of the other weapons they've crated up. They have an Army tractor and low boy trailer. I wonder if they have been reported missing. Let's go back to the base and and check the motor pool."

At the motor pool they checked with the duty sergeant.

"Transportation handles the big rigs, Sir. See Sgt. Mills, he can tell you what you want to know."

They thanked the sergeant and left for Transportation.

Sgt. Mills took them out in truck yard. "No semi or trailer has been checked out, Sir," he informed them. "but let's look around, I'll know in a minute if one is missing. There should be eleven tractors and three low boys."

They went through the yard.

"God damn it, there is one missing, a low boy and a jeep. That's what they hook on the rear for heavy loads. Son-of-a-bitch, when did they disappear? There's been no calls for the big ones so I haven't been checking. Now who the hell?"

"Looks like someone sneaked on out when you weren't looking."

"All these trucks have numbers on the door and on the trailers, too. I'll get them for you."

The number on the truck was 6-10. The trailer number was T7-1. Bronski called the Highway Patrol and asked them to relay the numbers to all states west of them.

Capt. Bowman, one of the investigators tacking the tractor and trailer, phoned Bronski that evening.

"This guy is heading west, Joe, but he keeps deviating north and south. He only travels early in the morning and late at night. He must be hiding out during the day. He stopped for gas at a little wide spot in the road in west Texas and charged it to the Army. The proprietor was fit to be tied when he found out the rig was stolen. I told him we'd try to get his money for him. He swung north after that and we lost him in New Mexico."

"OK, Jack, keep after him and keep me posted. No luck with the Air Force."

Hart called Fort Rycker to check on the agents there.

"We're holding two, Bret. We had your girl Carol in on it to lean on the girlfriend of one and the wife of an officer the other guy claims he spent the night with. Carol told her we'd keep it quiet if she told us the truth. That Carol's a pretty sharp gal, I know why you keep her around. What should we do with these two?"

"Hold them, Joe and I will be back in the morning."

At Fort Johns, Bronski and Hart got one of the corporals to talk after sweating him for three hours. Almost in tears, the young soldier talked.

"I didn't have any choice, they said they'd cut my throat if I didn't help them and give me a thousand dollars if I did. I still have the money."

"Who are they?"

He named the four men who were AWOL.

"Who else is involved in this beside them?"

"They'll kill me if I tell you," he sobbed.

"There's four men in the morgue, your buddies, how would you like to be charged with their murders?"

"No, no, I didn't have anything to do with that, I swear."

"OK, then talk."

He was sobbing so hard he could hardly talk. Bronski waited patiently.

"Gimme a break, Colonel, and I'll tell you."

"All right we'll do what we can."

"Captain Clarich, the Artillery officer, is head of the ring here, but there are others beside him that I don't know."

"Where are they taking the weapons?"

"I don't know exactly, from what I heard they're taking them out of the country."

"OK, Bret, let's put this guy on ice and go pick up the Captain."

Bronski, Bret, and two other agents checked around and found that Capt. Clarich was having lunch at the "O Club" with two fellow officers. They walked in, surrounded the table, and Bronski tapped Clarich on the shoulder.

"Would you please come with us, Captain?"

"What's this all about?"

"I'm sure you know, but we won't discuss it here."

"But I haven't finished my lunch."

"Forget it, get your cover and let's go." Bronski took a firm grip on his arm and lifted him out of the chair."

"You two be where we can get hold of you if necessary," said Hart.

At Col. Sorenson's Office they sat Clarich in a chair.

"Now, we can do this the easy way or the hard way, whichever you prefer."

"I don't know what you're talking about."

"I presume that means you want to do it the hard way. First I'm going to ask you some questions nice! If you don't cooperate, then we'll get tough. We know that you're the head of the weapons stealing ring here, so now we want to know where they're being taken."

"I still don't know what you're talking about."

"Have you ever heard of Sgt. MacMillan and Sgt. Boone at Fort Rycker?"

Clarich turned white and held his hands.

"What's the matter, Captain? You don't look well."

"No, no, I'm all right."

"Good, I'm going to have the sergeants come over here and question you. General. would you call Fort Rycker and have them fly the sergeants here?"

"Yes, Colonel." He picked up the phone and started to dial.

"No, oh God no, I'll talk." Hart put the phone down.

"You must have heard about the method the sergeants use to loosen tongues."

"For God's sake, you're mad."

"No, Captain, you're mad, whatever possessed you to get mixed up in something like this in the first place, and what made you think you could get away with it?"

The Captain broke down and put his head in his hands.

"They approached me and I needed money to pay off some gambling debts that the gamblers were leaning on me to pay. If I hadn't gone along I would have been killed by one or the other."

"Where are they taking the stuff? We've trailed that rig with the rocket launcher all the way to New Mexico."

"I don't know, someplace where they have a big landing area."

"You mean they're going to fly all those weapons out of the country?"

"Yes, but I don't know where they're going."

"Jesus, they'll need a damn big plane to take all that out of the country. They'll have to make it in one trip, they couldn't risk more than one flight. General, call Gen. Nickelsen and see if he knows of any big cargo planes missing, then call the FAA and see if they can run down any flights by big civilian transports not connected with a legitimate airline."

Hart picked up the phone and dialed a number.

"51st Air Recon Group, Sgt. Lane."

"Hello, Sergeant, this is Gen. Hart, is Gen. Nickelsen in?"

"Yes Sir, I'll connect you."

"Gen. Hart, how can I help you?"

"General, do you know of any big cargo planes that are missing?" He told him about the missing weapons.

"I don't know, but I can sure as hell find out real fast, do you want to hold on?" He put Hart on hold and had Sgt. Lane dial another number.

"Air Transport Command. Sgt. Jones."

"This is Sgt. Lane, calling Gen. Terry for Gen. Nickelsen."

"I'll connect you."

"Hello, Wayne, how are you?

"Fine, George, I need some information quick."

"What do you need, Wayne?"

"Do you have any large cargo planes missing?"

"We've got a C5 over due now, why do you ask?"

Gen. Nickelsen explained about the missing ordnance.

"Col. Bronski has learned that they're planning to fly the stuff out of the country, but right now he doesn't know from where."

"Well, that C5 would sure as hell do the job. We'll start checking on it right away and I'll get back to you as soon as I find out anything."

"Good, I'll be here in my office." He pushed the button for Gen. Hart. "Gen. Hart, I think I may have some information for you real soon. I just talked to Gen. Terry of the ATC and he told me they had a C5 overdue. He's checking on it right now and will get back to me as soon as he has any information on it, then I'll get right back to you. Where can I reach you?"

"I'm at Fort Johns, you can reach me at the Ordnance Depot." He gave him the number.

"What did you find out, Bret?" asked Bronski.

Hart briefed him on what he had learned.

"If they get hold of that C5 it would be big enough to haul all of their mid-night requisitions. What we have to find out is where the pick up point is."

"That rig is heading west. We should look for a place that's big enough to set a large plane down and take off again loaded. Let's go over to Operations and look at some charts."

"CHAPTER THREE"

The phone rang n Col. Sorenson's office. He picked it up. "Ordnance, Col. Sorenson."

"Hello, this is the OSI. Is Col. Bronski there?"

"Yes, mam, he's right here. It's for you, Colonel."

"Bronski here."

"Hello, Joe, I have Charley and the Chief on the line."

"Hello, Joe, I thought I'd kill two birds with one stone," said Charley, "I'm calling to let Frank know what's going on and to let you know what we found. We checked things out at Fort Lewis. They really got ripped off, three cases of M16's, three 50 cal. machine guns, five 60mm mortars, and two 75mm field pieces. They don't have a count on the ammunition yet."

"Are there any trucks missing?" asked Bronski.

"Yes, a five ton stake. It was seen heading west and then heading north. I have a couple of men trying to locate it. We're at MacKenzie now and almost the same deal. We know they got a bunch of ammo from both bases. We're getting ready to track this one."

"OK, we've tracked a semi hauling a rocket launcher, some weapons, and ammo all the way to New Mexico. The Air Force has a C5 missing. We were told that they're planning to fly the stuff out of the country. We're at Operations to look at some charts to see if we can figure out where they might be able to set down something that big and take off again. Keep checking with Mona and we'll keep her informed."

"OK, Joe, done, talk to you later."

"You fellows be careful," said Mona.

"OK, sweet, we will."

At Operations, a young sergeant got them some charts of everything west of Amarillo. Looking at the charts, Bronski deduced, "There's no place they could set a C5 down except at an air base or a civilian airport and they sure wouldn't chance that. It has to be someplace where they've stock piled the weapons."

"How about a highway? suggested Hart.

"Not likely, there's usually telephone poles, sign posts, or trees that they could hit with a wing. Those things have a hell of a droop to them when they're on the ground. On top of that a highway doesn't have a thick enough concrete to hold one of those babies and like I said, it has to be someplace where they've brought all the weapons together ready to load. It has to be in New Mexico or some place near, we've tracked the launcher that far."

The young sergeant that got the charts for them was standing nearby.

"Pardon me, Colonel, may I say something?"

"Yes, Sergeant, what is it?"

"Sir, I was raised around Rozwell, New Mexico and I know the country pretty well."

"What are you trying to tell us, Sergeant?"

"I think there's one place where they could land a C5."

"Where's that?"

"There's a ridge about forty or fifty miles northwest of Gallup. The top is flat for about three or three and a half miles. The ground is real solid and by clearing away the brush and rocks, it would make an ideal runway, long enough for a C5 to land and take off. There's a road to the top where a truck could easily make it up. I've been up there in a pickup hunting with no problem. Here, I'll show you on the chart. There, that ridge," he said, pointing it out to them.

"Good boy, you may just have the answer. Bret, call Biggs AFB and have them send a couple of planes over that area to see if they can spot anything."

A corporal came to the door.

"Gen. Hart?"

"That's me."

"I have a message for you, Sir." He handed Hart the message.

"It's from Gen. Nickelsen. He's heard from Gen. Terry. That C5 they're missing went off the radar screen over northern Arizona and they've lost contact with it. Two F16's are missing from Luke AFB."

"Have them get those planes from Biggs in the air fast,"

said Bronski. He picked up the phone and dialed OSI.

"Good afternoon, OSI."

"Joe, Mona, I've got some news for Charley." He gave her the information he had. "We're heading for Gallup, New Mexico as soon as we hear from Biggs AFB. Tell Charley to get out there as soon as he can."

"Got it, Joe, good luck and be careful."

The planes from Biggs came back and reported.

"We didn't see a thing, there's nothing there or they have it well camouflaged. There's a long flat area where they could land a plane, but we didn't see any."

"Let's jump in the 310 and fly out for a look ourselves," said Bronski. "Bret, see if you can get permission for the sergeant to come with us. Care to go for a ride, Sergeant? By the way, what's your name?"

"Sgt. Willard Buckman, Sir," he said grinning, "just give me five to grab my bag."

That night Bronski sat the 310 down on the runway at Gallup. In the FBO they inquired about renting a four wheel drive vehicle. The girl at the desk called and made the arrangements for the vehicles and their rooms for the night.

"Bret, Buckman and I will fly over the area in the morning and you two can take the four wheel drive to where the road leaves the black top to go to the top of the hill. If we see anything, we can come back and signal you to meet us on top."

At Luke AFB two pilots were found murdered. The day before two F16's had taken off and disappeared off the radar screen. There had been no sign of them since.

"CHAPTER FOUR"

The following morning the big King Air with Lt. Col. Blake and four agents landed at Gallup Airport. At the FBO Blake was told where he could contact Lt. Col. Bronski.

Thirty minutes later two four wheel drive vehicles pulled up to the FBO. Blake and his men joined Bronski and the others.

The two vehicles loaded and pulled out. Bronski, Hart, and Buckman took off in the 310. Buckman acting as guide pointed the way to Bronski.

"The road that leads to the top is about thirty miles farther on from here," said Buckman, "you'll be able to spot it easy from up here."

"We'll make a few passes over the top and then come down and let the others know what we find if anything."

Buckman pointed out the ridge as they approached it. They flew the entire length without seeing anything when suddenly Buckman pointed. "Look there, Colonel."

"Where? I don't see anything."

"There, near the end of the ridge, covered with camouflage netting.

"I still don't see it."

Buckman laughed. "I can see it because I'm color blind. Fly low and I'll tell you when to circle. Look like there's something under there."

When he circled again Bronski and Hart finally saw what Buckman was looking at.

"Well, I'll be damned, I see it now, let's land and take a good look."

Bronski set the plane down and taxied up to what looked like an enormous tent made out of netting. They got out and went inside. There were empty crates piled on the side and the semi with the trailer and two five ton stake trucks were in the rear.

"Hey, Colonel," called Buckman, "come over here."

Several men were sitting on the ground, bound and gagged. They untied one.

"Christ, am I glad to see you, those bastards tied us up and left us here to die. If you hadn't come along, we'd have had it. They took off not more than twenty minutes ago in our C5, loaded with all kinds of weapons. Those guys over there are part of the gang but they left them here with us and took off."

Four of the men were the crew of the C5. The other eight were AWOL soldiers from Fort Johns, Fort Lewis, Fort Rycker, and Fort MacKenzie.

"There's a couple of four wheel drive vans waiting to come up, I'd better take off and let them know what we found. I'll also get the State Police and have them pick up these guys. They can hold them until the MP"s can come get them."

Bronski called the FAA when he was airborne and had them contact Biggs AFB to scramble some planes to intercept the C5 before it got out of range. Then he landed on the highway near the vehicles.

"What did you find up there, Joe?" asked Blake.

"We hit the jackpot. The crew from the C5 and eight of the gang that stole the weapons and drove the truck. Their partners pulled a double cross and left them tied up with the C5 crew. I called the FAA to contact Biggs to scramble some planes to intercept the C5. Call the State Police on your radio and have them come pick up those eight and hold them for the MP's, then drive up on top. I'll take off and meet you there."

In the meantiime, Hart was questioning the men.

"I'm Capt. Wilken and this is my co-pilot, Lt Michaels. This is Lt. Newton, our navigator, and Lt. Peters our engineer."

"Did you happen to hear where they're taking those weapons?"

"Yes, Sir, Bolivia. It seems they're having a revolution or something down there."

Hart grabbed one of the men he recognized from Fort Rycker.

"Who's masterminding this operation?"

Silence--------

"We can get MacMlllan here to make you talk if that's what you want."

"OK, ok, I'll tell you, it's Col. Rodriguez."

"Rodriguez!" he exclaimed, surprised. "Has he been flying stuff here in that Beaver?"

"Yeah, for the past two months that I know of."

"Why that son-of-a-bitch, no wonder he made so many trips to see his family."

"That's how all the equipment got here to clear the runway for the C5 and the F16's to land. It's all back there."

"We'll make arrangements to get you guys back to your bases then I can't guarantee what they'll do to you. There's murder charges waiting for some of you. Capt. Wilkens, Col. Bronski will make some provisions to get you back to your base. How did they manage to get the C5 away from you?"

"They were on board to take care of some cargo and they jumped us in mid-air and took over. Two of them are suppose to be ex-bomber pilots and the other two are suppose to be ex-fighter pilots, but I never heard of them. When I found out who they were, I remembered that they had dishonorable discharges from the Air Force. They loaded the F16's in the C5 with the other weapons from here.

Bronski landed and a while later the two four wheel drives arrived.

Hart walked up to Bronski. "Joe, you won't believe who Mr. Big is in this operation."

"Who?'

"Col. Rodriguez. he's been flying shipments of stuff in here in the Beaver for the past two months at least. This is where his 'family' is."

"Why that bastard. Charley, I'll fly you back to Gallup, then will you go down to Biggs and see how they're making out intercepting the C5? I want to get on the horn to Rycker and have Rodriguez picked up, then Bret, Buckman and I will fly back there. You can come back here to pick up your boys and get them home. They can wait here for the State Police to pick up these prisoners then meet you in Gallup. I'll call ATC to send a plane to Gallup for Wilkens and his crew.

As soon as he landed at Gallup, Bronski went in the office and called Fort Rycker.

"Fort Rycker Army Base, Sgt. Dean."

"This is Col. Bronski, will you connect me with Security?"

"Yes, Sir, Colonel."

"Col. Hansen speaking."

"Col. Hansen, this is Col. Bronski."

"Hello, Colonel, what can I do for you?"

"I want you to take Col. Rodriguez in custody as soon as I hang up."

"Col. Rodriguez? Are you serious?"

"Never more serious in my life. Now, I would appreciate it if you would get right on it."

"Gotcha, Colonel, consider it done."

"Good, I'll be taking off for Rycker in about thirty minutes and should be in there this evening." He broke the connection.

Hansen picked up his mic and called his MP's.

"All available units, pick up Col. Rodriguez and bring him to Security headquarters."

"Col. Hansen, this is unit two. Col. Rodriguez took off in his Beaver not more than fifteen minutes ago and headed west."

Hansen reached for the phone.

"Get me Houston Center of the FAA, quick!"

"This is Col. Hansen, Fort Rycker Security. A Beaver just took off from here about fifteen minutes ago heading west. Can you pick him up on radar? The pilot is a fugitive and must be apprehended. Can you help us?"

160

"Give us a little time, Colonel, and we'll call you back. There shouldn't be any problem."

Two hour later Hansen's phone rang.

"Col. Hansen, here."

"Col. Hansen, this is Houston Center. We've located your Beaver and have scrambled two F4's from Bergstrom AFB to intercept him. They're on him now and are attempting to force him to land either at Houston-Ellington or Bergstrom AFB. The MP's will take him into custody if he lands at the base and the local police have been notified if he lands at Houston. They'll let you know where he'll be."

"Thank you very much for your assistance, I'll be waiting for the call."

"Anytime, Colonel, glad to be of service."

"CHAPTER FIVE"

When Bronski landed at Fort Rycker, Col. Hansen was waiting for him at the air strip.

"Hello, Col. Bronski. They have Col. Rodriguez in custody at Berstrom AFB. He took off in the Beaver before we could apprehend him so I called Houston Center and they picked him up on radar. They called Bergstrom AFB and had them send up a couple of F4's to force him to land. They herded him over to the base and made him land. The MP's took him into custody."

Bronski laughed. "Good work, Colonel. I'll bet we've given the Air Force more excitement in the past few days than they've had in months. I'll arrange for gas and we'll go after him in the morning. Come on, Buckman, we'll treat you to a steak and get you a room in the NCBOQ."

"Before you go, Colonel, there's a call for you from Col. Blake. Call Communications, they have the message."

The message was to call Biggs AFB. Bronski had the operator put through the call.

"Biggs Operations, Sgt. Berhens."

"This is Col. Bronski, can you locate Col. Blake for me?"

"Yes, Sir, he's right here."

"Joe, we've got the C5 on the ground and the crew in cuffs. The F16's had to chase him out over the gulf before they caught up to him. He wasn't going to turn back, but they told him they had orders to blow him out of the sky if he didn't return to Biggs. I guess they were convincing."

"Give those F16 boys my 'well done'."

"I will, Joe. When the plane landed the MP's took the crew to the stockade. The pilot, co-pilot, and two other pilots are all ex-Air Force with dishonorables. A couple of the others on the plane were South Americans. We haven't been able to get anything out of them yet."

"Have them keep a guard on the plane and make arrangements to have it and the F16's returned to their bases. It will have to be unloaded and the cargo shifted to smaller planes. None of the bases have runways long enough to handle the C5."

"OK, I'll make arrangements to get these guys back to Rycker and then we can get the truth out of them."

"Rodriguez took off in the Beaver before they could nab him, but Hansen had the sense to call Houston Center and they put a couple of F4's from Bergstrom on him. He's at the base and as soon as I'm gassed up in the morning we'll go after him."

"All right, I'll take care of everything here and start back in the morning."

"I'll bet the Old Man is jumping up and down because we haven't let him know what's been going on," laughed Hart.

"Hell, things have been happening too fast. Do you want to go see him now?"

"No, let him stew for awhile. When we get back with Rodriguez we can go see him. He'll probably want to court martial both of us," laughed Hart.

When Bronski, Hart, and Buckman picked up Rodriguez at Bergstrom AFB he became indignant.

"What is the meaning of this Gen. Hart?" he demanded.

"Stow it, Rodriguez, we know all about your operation. We have the C5 with all your toys under guard at Biggs AFB and all your underdogs in custody. We'll get the rest of the story from you when we get back to Fort Rycker," said Hart. "Get in the rear seat and shut up. If he gets too mouthy, Sergeant, belt him one, You won't get in trouble for hitting an officer because he isn't one anymore."

"Is it necessary for me to be in handcuffs?"

"That's the way we treat all criminals. Don't worry about handcuffs, worry about the rope they're going to put around your neck."

Bronski put the 310 gently down on the runway at Fort

Rycker and was met by the "Follow Me" jeep that led him to the parking tarmac. Two cars full of MP's were there to take the prisoner into custody.

"Stuff him in the stockade and we'll be back after we see Gen. Harris. You might as well stick around and see the last act of the show, Sergeant. Make yourself comfortable until we get back."

Buckman grinned. "Thanks, Colonel, it's been real fun so far."

Capt. Fitch opened the door to Gen. Harris' office.

"Gen. Hart and Col. Bronski are here, Sir."

"Get them in here!" he bellowed. "Where in the hell have you two been and what have you been doing?"

Hart and Bronski smiled. "Sir," said Bronski, "if you would have us over for cocktails by your lovely wife and one of your delicious steaks, we could sit down and tell you all about it," said Bronski, with a grin.

The General started to sputter then relaxed and began to laugh.

"Bronski, you have got to be the most ballsy son-of-a-bitch I have ever had the pleasure to run across, but I'll say this, you get the job done. OK, you've got an invitation. How many will there be?"

"About twenty six if my boss and Mona come."

He sat upright. "What! Oh hell, all right, but this had better be good. I assume you two have got this all wrapped up or you wouldn't be so cocky."

Bronski and Hart laughed.

"Yes, Sir, we'll give you a rough briefing now and then tonight we can sit down in your study with Gen. Miner and kill two birds with one swat by enjoying your good brandy and giving you both the full details."

Gen. Harris shook his head and laughed.

"All right, can I figure on cocktails at 1800 hours?"

"I'm sure you can. First of all we want to tell you that

we've recovered all of the weapons and ammunition. They're sitting in a C5 at Biggs AFB, under guard. We're pretty sure we have all that were involved, including the ring leader."

"Alright, I'll see you at 1800 hours." He called to Fitch. "Fitch, round up five more grills for me and briquettes to go with them. Have them at my house and set up by 1600 hours. You're invited, too."

"Yes, Sir, General," he said with one of his rare smiles.

"CHAPTER SIX"

Bronski and Hart went back to security to question Rodriguez. he was sitting in his cell with his head in his hands. The guard unlocked the door.

"Come with us, Rodriguez, we have some questions."

"I have nothing to say to you."

They took him in a room and sat him at a table.

"Do you want to do this nice or would you rather we get nasty? Which way do you prefer?"

Silence------------

"Four men were killed at Fort Johns and two were murdered at Luke AFB. Since you were the brains of this operation, you will be held responsible for all six murders."

"I had nothing to do with that."

"How come you were stealing weapons for Bolivia?"

"I told you I had nothing to do with it."

"I guess you would rather we get nasty. General, why don't you send for Sgts. MacMillan and Boone? Maybe they can convince Mr. Rodriguez to talk. You do know the sergeants, don't you Rodriguez?"

He turned pale. "You wouldn't do that."

"You know, that's what everyone says just before we start. You must admit it's a very effective way of getting information, don't you think?"

Hart left the room and soon returned with Mac and Pat.

"Hello, Sergeants. Do you have your bag of tricks with you, Sgt. MacMillan?"

"Sure do, Colonel." He sat the bag on the table and began to remove the contents. No sooner had he driven the nails in the table, Rodriguez broke down.

"No, no, no, not that, I'll tell you."

"All right, we'll start with who gives you your orders?"

"My brother, he's head of the rebel army in Bolivia. With those weapons he could have overthrown the government and been the new Presidente. I would have become the

166

Commander of the Army. I was heading for Mexico when I was apprehended."

"How did you get all those men on those other bases to do your dirty work?"

"Offer a man enough money and he'll double cross his own mother. I've been setting this up for six months. All we had to do was find the men that needed money. A little threatening helped, too."

"Maybe some men can be bought, Rodriguez, but not all of them. We want the names of every man that's in this with you."

He gave them the names of the men at Fort Lewis, Fort Johns, Fort MacKenzie, and Fort Rycker. The two men that Carol and the agents tripped up and three others at Fort Rycker were on the list. They also got the names of the men at Luke AFB.

Bronski contacted Security Officers at the other three bases and gave them the names of the men to be picked up. A call to Luke AFB Security resulted in the arrest of three men that helped in the theft of the F16's and the murder of the two pilots.

At 1730 hours a Cessna Citation entered the traffic pattern at Fort Rycker then turned on the final approach path to the runway. It touched down gently on the concrete. It rolled to where the "Follow Me" jeep was waiting to lead the pilot to the parking tarmac. The pilot expertly swung the big aircraft into the tiedown space and as the ground crewman drew his finger across his throat, cut the engines.

When the engines wound down the door opened and Gen. Hart's face lit up as Mona Ferguson appeared in the opening. The stairs were lowered by the ground crewman and Bret reached up to take her hand as she descended. She ignored his hand and her arms went around his neck. Her lipstick left the outline of her lips on his.

Bret turned red. "That's for taking such good care of Joe."

Frank Miner appeared in the doorway and waved.

167

"Hello, Joe, and you, too, Bret, as soon as you get untangled from that girl you have in your arms."

With one arm still around Mona, Bret saluted.

"Hello, Sir, good to see you."

"Mona tells me I'm in for a treat, best cocktails and steaks anywhere."

"She got that right, Sir. If you have a special drink just tell Emily and she'll make it for you. The General's steaks are famous."

"It sounds like it will be a memorable evening."

"It will be, Chief. Charley should be flying in here any minute now," said Bronski.

"Why don't I drive Mona around and show her some of the base? We'll be able to see Charley when he comes in," suggested Bret.

"That's as good an excuse as any to get Mona alone," laughed Bronski.

"I'd love it," laughed Mona. She hooked her arm is his and they walked to the car.

"I'm never going to wash my face again," smiled Bret, as he touched his lips.

"CHAPTER SEVEN"

Six cars pulled up in front of Gen. Harris' house. Lt. Col. Bronski and twenty five people, including Sr M/Sgt. MacMillan, Sr M/Sgt. Boone, and Sgt. Buckman, emerged. Emily Harris met them at the door.

"Hello, Mona, how nice that you could come, I was hoping you would."

"I'm happy to be here," she said as they embraced.

"Emily, I'd like you to meet our commander, Gen. Frank Miner." Gen. Miner bowed and took her hand then raised it to his lips.

"So you are the fabulously beautiful Emily Harris I have heard so many wonderful things about. Please call me Frank."

"Bret, you must stop bringing these fantastic men here, my heart just won't stand it." She fluttered her eyelashes at Frank.

"Oh, brother," moaned Bret, smiling inwardly. Both Emily and Frank burst out laughing. She hooked her arm in his and led them into the house.

"Come in, Frank. What would you like to drink? In fact what would all of you like? When you introduce yourselves, tell me what your pleasure is."

"I've been told about your fantastic talent for mixing drinks, surprise me," said Frank.

"Very well, I know just what you would like."

As each introduced themselves they gave her their choice of drink, firing their orders at her. Charley watched with interest.

"She's bound to screw this up," he said to himself.

Emily busied herself setting up glasses and mixing drinks. When she had all the drinks mixed and lined up on the bar, she called each one's name and handed them their drink. "Here you are, Gentlemen, and Lady, cheers."

"Did everyone get the right drink?" asked Charley.

Everyone affirmed. He raised his glass, "A toast to the Queen of the Bar!"

They all chimed in, "Hear! Hear!"

"Emily, you never cease to amaze me, how do you do it?" asked Charley.

"I have an alcoholic memory," she said laughing, "what I do is dazzle them with my beauty and they forget what they"re drinking." Everyone roared with laughter.

"Ouch! That's the worst one yet, Emily," moaned Bret.

"Now that I have you all in a happy mood, let's retire to the patio and pay our respects to the backyard chef."

Gen. Harris was busy tending six grills that were loaded with steaks.

"Greetings, Lady and Gentlemen, I'm George Harris for those of you who haven't met me before. How do you like your steaks? Right now they're just about approaching the rare stage, so sing out."

Each guest introduced themselves and ordered their steaks.

"George, I'd like you to meet our commander, Gen. Frank Miner," said Bronski.

"I'm very pleased to meet you, Frank. I've heard a lot about you."

"It's a pleasure to finally meet you, George. I've just been amazed at your wife's fantastic talents and I'm told I'll get the same reaction here from your famous steaks."

"Yes, it's tough having two geniuses in the same household," he said laughing. Frank joined him.

"We'll get together with Bret and Joe after dinner."

"Mona came up. "Hello, George, how's my favorite chef?"

"Just fine, and if you'll let go of that young man's arm, I'll give you a hug."

"You and Frank should get along fine, you're both bullies," she said laughing.

Frank and George laughed as he gave her a hug.

"Can I give you a hand with the cooking, George?" asked Frank.

"This is the biggest order I've ever tackled, it's a challenge, but I think I can handle it. Thanks anyhow."

Master Sergeant Carol Man walked in. When Bronski saw her he immediately went to take her arm.

"Well, you're a sight for sore eyes, I didn't think you were going to show up."

"Better late than never," she said looking up and smiling.

"Come on, I'd like you to meet my boss."

They went over to Frank and George.

"I don't believe I've met this young lady," said George.

"This Carol Man, George. Carol, you know Gen. Harris.

"Good evening, General."

"How do you do and it's George for tonight."

"Carol, this is Gen. Frank Miner, my boss."

"Hello, Carol. I heard you played an important roll in helping to solve our recent dilemma."

"Oh, I did help a little."

"Don't be so modest, Carol, you helped a lot."

Bret and Mona walked up.

"Mona, I'd like you to meet Master Sergeant Carol Man, she works with me."

"Hello, Carol. You must be the one that's got Joe's adrenaline flowing."

"Hi, Mona, I hope I'm doing as good a job on Joe as you are on Gen. Hart."

"No telling tales out of school, Carol," smiled Bret.

"I'm sorry, Carol, I didn't recognize you without your stripes," said George.

"Carol is my girl Friday, George," smiled Bret.

"Of course, I should have recognized you. Again, sorry."

When they finished their steaks, Bronski said to Gen. Harris, "Sir, would you like to join Gen. Miner, Gen. Hart, Col. Blake, and me in your study? We'll give you a complete rundown on the activities of the past several days."

"Excellent idea. Come on, Frank, let's see what these boys have been up to. The study is the only room in the house where Emily will let me enjoy a good cigar. She

171

even put an air purifier in here. I also have an excellent bottle of brandy tucked away in my desk.

For the next two hours Bronski, Hart, and Blake gave them a complete rundown on their activities.

"I'll start where Bret and I left your office on the day I arrived at Fort Rycker. Our first stop was the Ordnance Depot. We had Gen. Hoyt get all the men that worked for him in the depot and began questioning them. Bret had a couple of his men and I called in a few more to check their stories. That was where Carol came in. A couple of the stories involved females so Carol questioned them to check the men's stories. She proved to be an asset.

"We got the size and weights of the stolen pieces as well as the size and weights of the ammunition containers. Our next step was to check the gate guards and their logs. We found that some trucks had gone out with crates and boxes, but the guards just checked the bills of lading and not the contents of the boxes and crates. We put men checking the destination and receivers. We didn't fare so well with that.. Bret issued an order to the guards that in the future all crates and boxes would be opened for inspection. You had met all the men I brought in except Major Nelson. They all helped us with "Operation Boom" if you recall."

Gen. Harris smiled at the nomenclature.

"If you recall you had a call from Gen. Minten at Fort Johns. The next morning Bret and I flew over and met with the General. We had no sooner arrived when he informed us that Fort Lewis and Fort MacKenzie both had been victimized. I got on the phone and called the office for Charley and asked him to take some men and start the investigation there.

"Among the other weapons, which will be listed in our report, a rocket launcher was taken from Fort Johns and the crew murdered. The base had been out on maneuvers so the weapons were stolen before they could be returned to the Fort. We immediately called for more men to track the launcher, figuring it would be the hardest piece to conceal.

"The thieves had also stolen a large quantity of lumber and stopped on the way to build a box around the launcher and crate some of the other weapons. The tractor and low boy trailer they loaded it on for hauling was stolen from the Fort. Our men tracked it all the way to New Mexico, but then they lost it. This puzzled us at the time, but soon we found out why.

"From one of the men we questioned at Fort Johns, we learned they were going to fly the weapons out of the county. We figured they would need a large cargo plane to haul all their loot at one time so we check with the Air Force and learned that a C5 was missing. Also that two F16's were missing from Luke AFB. Later we learned that two pilots at Luke had been murdered.

"At Fort Johns Operations we looked at some charts to see if we could find a place for a C5 to land and take off. Fortunately for us, the young sergeant you met tonight, Sgt. Willard Buckman, was standing near and overheard what we were looking for. He told us he had been raised around Rozwell, N.M. and knew a ridge northwest of Gallup that had a flat top and was big enough to handle a C5.

"We flew out there with some men and arranged for some four wheel drive vans. Bret, Buckman, and I flew over the area, but didn't see a thing until Buckman, who is color blind, spotted the camouflage netting that was covering something. I landed and we checked it out. Under the netting were the C5 crew and eight of the gang members all bound and gagged. The C5 with all the weapons had taken off about fifteen minutes before we arrived.

"Charley had flown in that morning and was with the men in the vehicles. I called the FAA and had them notify Biggs AFB to scramble some planes to intercept the C5. I then landed on the highway, told Charley what we had found, and sent them on to the top. Charley went back to Gallup with a couple of men and flew to Biggs to check on the progress of the interceptors. The fighters caught up to the C5 and forced it to return to Biggs where it is now with all the weapons and ammunition intact.

"By questioning the gang members on the mountain, we learned that they were planning to fly the weapons to Bolivia. We also learned that Col. Rodriguez was the brains behind the operation."

"Why that son-of-a-bitch!" exclaimed Gen. Harris.

"I called Col. Hansen at Security and instructed him to take Rodriguez into custody, then Bret, Buckman, and I flew back here. When we landed we were informed that Rodriguez had taken off in the Beaver about twenty minutes before I called and was seen heading west. Col. Hansen had the presence of mind to call the FAA at Houston Center and had them pick him up on radar.

"They contacted Bergstrom AFB and had them scramble a couple of F4's to intercept him. They forced him to land at the base where he was taken into custody by the MP's. We took off the next morning and brought him back. He's now in the stockade.

"By questioning him we found out his brother is the head of the rebel army and is trying to overthrow the government so he can be the next Presidente. Rodriguez would have become the Commander In Chief of the Army. He gave us the names of all the men that were involved and we now have them all in custody. The men that helped steal the F16's and murder the pilots are also in custody.

"It will take a few days to put the full report together and catalogue the evidence so I would appreciate if you could spare Gen. Hart to come to Fort Clark and work with me on the details."

Gen. Harris smiled. "I suppose he will be working rather close with Mona to get this accomplished?"

"Why yes, Sir, he'll be spending a lot of time with Mona."

Gen. Hart tried to hide his grin.

"Very well, I suppose I could do without him for a week or so."

"Thank you, Sir, we should have the complete report for you in a few days but it will take a few weeks to put all the evidence together for the prosecutors."

"I don't suppose you would want Sgt. Man to help Mona type those reports and keep all the documents straight?"

Bronski grinned. "Yes, Sir, that is an excellent idea, we could sure use her."

"Bret, seeing as how she's one of your people, you take care of that."

"Yes, Sir, I'll have her orders made out transferring her to the OSI for an indefinite period. She can fly back with us in the morning."

"Well Frank, all I can say is these three have done one hell of a job and we can't thank them enough."

"Not only us, General, but everyone out there enjoying your steaks and whiskey played an important part in solving and wrapping up this case. Not only them, but the Air Force pilots who forced the C5 to return to Biggs and the F4's that caught up with Rodriguez and forced him to land at Bergstrom, they played an important part. If it hadn't been for Sgt. Buckman knowing the country out there we would never have found out where they were taking off from until it was too late to catch them. That was the one really important break in the case. It's just too bad that four men at Fort Johns and the two pilots at Luke AFB had to lose their lives."

"This just might earn you those silver eagles on your shoulder, Joe. You, too, Charley. It's certainly going to earn a Meritorious Service decoration for all of you," smiled Frank.

"I'll sign that recommendation," said George. "Right now I think there's a beautiful young lady and her beautiful new partner from OSI out there that need a little romancing, so get out of here."

Bret and Joe both stood up and saluted. "YES, SIR!" they chorused, and headed for the door.

"I think I should go out there and make sure those ladies are being treated properly," laughed Charley.

The General chuckled. "You're all excused so Frank and I can enjoy a good cigar and some fine brandy." He turned to Frank. "Did I ever tell you-------------------------------------."

Frank smiled and leaned back to swirl and sniff his brandy.

"General, did anyone ever accuse you of playing cupid?" smiled Frank.

George had a sly grin on his face.

"CHAPTER EIGHT"

The next morning Bronski took off in the 310 for Fort Clark. His co-pilot (in name only) was a beautiful dark haired young lady with a dazzling smile. She was all eyes since this was the first time she had ever been in anything smaller than a DC3, and had never been in the cockpit of a plane before. She was fascinated by the ease with which Bronski handled the twin engine aircraft.

As soon as he was on course and at his assigned altitude, he flipped on the auto-pilot then reached over and kissed her on the cheek. She looked at him and smiled.

"Not that I'm adverse to your affections, but shouldn't you be flying this thing?"

"Actually I have a little man in that black box (pointing to the auto-pilot switch) that takes over when I have more important things to attend to."

She turned and looked at Bret and Mona.

"Well, if Mona and the General aren't worried, there's no need for me to." She leaned over and kissed him.

For the next two days Joe and Carol worked together getting the report out, leaving Mona free to be with Bret.

On the third morning Bronski walked into Gen. Miner's office and laid the completed report on his desk. He looked at the front of the folder and smiled at the title. It read, "Operation Find A Gun". "Bronski humor," he remarked to himself.

He looked up at Bronski and smiled.

"I don't suppose you'll be needing the General and Sgt. Man any longer?"

"Oh yes, Sir, for at least another two weeks. We'll have to get all the evidence together for the prosecutors and after that at least another two weeks for the Sergeant and me to straighten up my office. All this paper work has made a mess out of it."

Miner looked up with a sly smile.

"I'm sure it will be immaculate when you're finished. Now get out of here and take care of that young lady."

He opened the report and began to read.

"Operation Find A Gun"

The case of the missing ordnance has been solved, details are as follows:

All missing weapons and ammunition have been recovered, including one C5, Two F16's, one tractor semi, one low boy trailer, and two five ton stake trucks, all Army property with the exception of the three aircraft.

All individuals involved in the thefts have been taken into custody and are presently being arraigned for trial. It is certain that with all the evidence against them, they will be found guilty and receive punishment befitting their crime.

The demoted Col. Rodriguez, the ring leader, has twice tried to commit suicide. He faces either a firing squad or a hanging if found guilty, which is a certainty.

A vote of thanks to S/Sgt. Willard Buckamn for his invaluable assistance on this case.

A vote of thanks to the F16 pilots that forced the C5 to return to Biggs AFB and the F4 pilots that forced Rodriguez to land at Bergstrom AFB.

Complete details are enclosed.

End of report,
Signed

Joseph Bronski, Lt. Col.
Special Investigator
Office of Special Investigations
United States Army

JB:cm

Copies to:
Gen. George Harris, Comdr. Fort Rycker
Gen. Howard Minten, Comdr. Fort Johns
Gen. Lawrence Bell, Comdr. Fort Lewis
Gen. Wallace Brady, Comdr. Fort MacKenzie

Gen. Wayne Nickelsen, Comdr. 51st Air Recon Gp.
Gen. Alfred Hicks, Comdr. Luke AFB
Gen. Eugene Moore, Comdr. Bergstrom AFB
Gen. Ralph Ryan, Comdr. Biggs AFB
Gen. George Terry, Comdr. ATC
Gen. Bret Hart, Chief of Staff, Fort Rycker

The next morning Bronski found an official-looking envelope on his desk. He opened it.

"Alright!" he exclaimed.

Gen. Frank Miner walked in smiling. In his hand was a pair of silver eagles. "These were mine, I'd be proud if you'd wear them."

"Thanks Frank, I'll be the one that will be proud."

That evening he whispered in Carol's ear, "You look much better in an evening gown than you do in a uniform."

They glided around the dance floor, holding her tight.

Sitting at the table watching and holding hands were Mona Ferguson and Bret Hart.

"Looks like Joe has finally found someone he really enjoys being with, present company accepted," smiled Mona. They moved together and touched cheeks.

The next morning Bronski's phone rang.

"Sgt. Buckman is on the line, Joe."

"Hello, Sergeant, how's things?"

"Hello, Colonel, just great. I heard about your promotion and wanted to congratulate you."

"Thank you Sergeant, that was thoughtful of you."

"I also wanted to thank you for the good time and the extra stripe I just got."

"Great, then congratulations to you, too, you earned it."

"Well, I just wanted to thank you for getting it for me."

"Hell, what's the use of being a Colonel if you can't throw your weight around a little," he said laughing.

"Right, but I'm glad you threw it in my direction. Any time I can do anything for you, just holler, Sir."

"Thanks, T/Sergeant, I'll remember, take care, so long."

PART FOUR

"Operation Foiled Mission"

"OPERATION FOILED MISSION"

New Orleans, 2 May

Barbara Jackson, undercover agent for OSI, working as a maid on the fourth floor of the Sheraton New Orleans Hotel, received a call from the front desk informing her that there were four Libyan and four Iraqi men checking in and would be occupying, 404, 406, 408, and 410, all adjoining rooms.

Barbara quickly went in each room and installed a bug. These were a very unique and highly technical electronic devices, designed by Doc Nagle, the electronics wizard for OSI. They replaced the regular light switch cover and could pick up conversation for over twenty feet, clearly, filtering out all other noises except voices. These looked like any other light switch cover, but were undetectable. In the maid closet down the hall, Barbara hooked up four separate tape recorders, one for each room, that recorded only the conversation in that room. Another of Doc's inventions.

As soon as the men entered the room the bugs picked up their voices and the recorders, voice activated, recorded the conversation, which was all in Arabic.

Barbara could only understand a few words that were said, but what little she did get was enough for her to surmise that these men were terrorists. She let the tapes run for about two hours, then quickly removing and placing them in her purse, she replaced them with fresh ones.

She called housekeeping and told them she would be gone for awhile, then hurried down to the French Quarter to another agent, Jean Paul Napier. Sauntering along, looking like tourist, she stepped into the souvenir shop next to the Saint Louis Hotel. Two ladies were in there looking over the merchandise. When she had a chance and would not be noticed, she slipped into the back room.

Jean Paul Napier, born of French parents, a native of New Orleans, thirty-one years old, five feet nine, one hundred sixty five pounds, black wavey hair, gray green eyes, handsome features, and a pencil thin mustache.

His parents were wealthy Louisiana plantation owners. He attended Columbia University, majoring in languages and attaining a Masters Degree. After graduating he went abroad to continue his study of languages. Among the twenty odd languages he mastered was Arabic, which he spoke and wrote fluently.

Barbara Ellen Jackson, thirty one years old, five feet eight, one hundred fifteen pounds, trim figure, black hair, dark brown eyes, pearly teeth, light brown complexion, and attractive features. Her mother was French and a talented musician. Her father was French and Negroid, and a highly respected attorney with offices in Baton Rouge.

Barbara graduated from Louisiana University with a bachelor's degree in Psychology, then went to Cornell University to obtain a law degree. She joined the Army shortly after graduating and upon completion of her basic training, was sent to Officer's school.

Her first assignment was with the Inspector General's office. Her work there was so impressive that after two years she was recommended to the OSI by her superiors and was promoted to the rank of Captain. She worked with several investigators and did such outstanding work that (then) Col. Miner sent her to New Orleans to be assistant head of that office under Jean Paul Napier.

The rear of the shop was set up as the headquarters of the OSI. Barbara briefed him quickly and handed him the tapes. He placed them on the machine, put a headset on, and handed another set to Barbara.

He turned on the machine and his electric typewriter at the same time and as the tape played he typed out the translation. Barbara shook her head in amazement.

"I wish those damn Arabs wouldn't all talk at once, it would be a lot easier to translate," he complained.

The tapes revealed that the men were indeed terrorists. They were making plans to place bombs in state and federal buildings, assassinate a number of government officials, import a large amount of counterfeit twenty dollar bills, and a large shipment of drugs.

"I think Gen. Miner should see this right away," said Jean Paul. He fed the typewritten translation into the cryptograph machine then sent it on to the OSI headquarters at Fort Clark.

"Good work, Barb," he said, patting her on the shoulder, "I think you had better get back to the hotel. Try to get in their rooms and find something that will tell us where they plan to place bombs and who they intend to assassinate. Hell, why am I telling you this, you know what to do. The minute you get anything you think is important, rush it to me." He gave her a squeeze and kissed her cheek. "Above all, be careful."

"I will, Jean Paul. My tapes are running so there should be something on them that's important."

"OK, I'm going to keep sending this stuff to headquarters and make them aware of what's happening."

"CHAPTER TWO"

OSI Headquarters, Fort Clark, 2 May

Mona Ferguson heard the cryptograph machine and went to get the message. When the tape was finished she ran it through the decoder. When she saw what was on the tape she hurried into her boss, Brig. Gen. Frank Miner.

"Get a load of this, Chief, it looks like we could be in for a bunch of trouble."

He read the message and looked up.

"Christ Almighty, is Joe in his office?"

"Yes Sir, I'll ring him." She picked up the phone and dialed Col. Bronski's office.

"Joe, Mona, can you come to Frank's office right away?"

"On my way."

Bronski rapped twice and entered.

Miner looked up. "Come in, Joe, and take a look at this."

He handed him the message. Bronski read it and emitted a low whistle.

"Damn Chief, we'd better get on this fast. I assume this came from Barbara via Jean Paul. I'm sure she's staying on top of it to get all the information she can. I'll take a couple of men and get down there. I also think we should contact the Vice-president and make him aware of this, we'll need all the support we can get. The FBI and the Secret Service should be alerted to get some protection for these officials and especially the President."

"Mona, get the Vice-president for me, please?"

Mona dialed the number.

"Good morning, this is the office of the Vice-president, Byron speaking."

"Good morning Byron, this is Mona Ferguson . Is the Vice-president in? Gen. Miner would like to talk to him."

"Yes, Miss Mona, I'll connect you."

She handed the phone to Frank.

"Good morning, Frank, what can I do for you?"

"Good morning George, I think we are about to have some serious problems. I'd like to send Col. Bronski over to you with the information we have so far."

"Alright, Frank, I'll be waiting for him."

"Thanks, George," The connection was broken.

When Bronski walked in Byron got up and rapped twice on the Vice-president's door then opened it.

"Col. Bronski is here, Sir."

He opened the door for him then closed it.

"Good morning, Colonel, what's up?"

"Good morning, Mr. Vice-president. We just got this message from our New Orleans office. I think you should read it." He handed him a copy of the original message.

He read it an looked up at Bronski.

"Do you think thiis is for real?"

"Yes, Sir, I do. But whether it is or not I don't think we should ignore it, there's too many lives at stake. As soon as I get back to the office I'm leaving for New Orleans with some more agents."

"Very well, Colonel, tell me what you want from me?"

"We'll need carte blanc authority to draw whatever resources we'll deem necessary to combat these people. Right now I don't know what we'll need and won't know until I get down there. I just need to know it's there if and when we need it. We have two agents down there and they're staying on top of it. I'll keep you informed through our office of what we're doing. In the meantime, if you would see that the President and the rest of the officials here in Washington are provided with sufficient protection, that would be a step ahead. That would include you, Sir."

"Good enough, Colonel. In the meantime I think this will take care of anything that you might need,"

He took a sheet of paper out of his drawer, picked up his pen, and began to write. When he finished he handed it to Bronski.

"That will give you the authority to draw on any help or anything else you need with no questions or arguments."

Bronski glanced at it and smiled.

"Thank you, Sir," he said extending his hand as he stood, "it's good to know we have your support."

"I wish you a lot of luck, Colonel," he replied as they shook hands.

On the way out Bronski stopped at Byron's desk, picked up the phone, and dialed his office.

"Good morning, OSI."

"Hi, Mona, Joe, I'm just leaving. Would you round up Gutterman and Bender? Tell them to be ready to leave as soon as I get back."

"OK, Joe, how'd it go with the V.P.?"

"Good, he's behind us all the way. I'll see you in a little bit."

When Bronski arrived at the office, Gutterman and Bender were waiting for him.

"I'll be right with you, boys. Mona, call Conley at the Treasury Dept. Tell them about the counterfeit money and to get someone down there to work with us. Make some reservations for us at the Sheraton and tell him to have his men contact us there. I'll keep you posted and I told the Vice-president I would keep him informed through you."

"Good luck Joe, and be careful."

"I will, sweetie."

"CHAPTER THREE"

New Orleans - 1500 hours.

Bronski tuned in his radio to 120.6, New Orleans Lakefront Airport Approach and keyed the mic.

"Lakefront Approach, this is Army 35 Bravo, twenty five northeast, landing Lakefront, we have information India."

"Army 35 Bravo, squawk 0426, say type aircraft."

"35 Bravo, a King Air, squawking 0426."

"35 Bravo radar contact, make straight in runway 18 Left."

"35 Bravo rog (roger), straight in 18 left."

"Army 35 Bravo, you are five miles out, contact tower on 119.9, good day."

"35 Bravo, good day." "Lakefront tower, 35 Bravo with you."

"35 Bravo cleared to land 18 Left."

"35 Bravo rog, cleared to land."

Bronski sat the big King Air down gently on the runway just past the numbers and slowed to make the turn on taxiway Juliet.

"35 Bravo, if able, turn left on Juliet and contact Ground on point seven."

"35 Bravo rog." He switched frequencies to ground control, 121.7. "Lakefront Ground, Amy 35 Bravo on Juliet."

"35 Bravo follow the jeep to parking. Welcome to New Orleans."

"35 Bravo rog."

A jeep with a checkered flag met him at the turn off and led him to transient parking.

Bronski swung the King Air into the tiedown space indicated by the ground crewman and shut down his engines at the signal. He performed his post flight check and exited the aircraft behind Gutterman and Bender.

"Welcome to the Sunny South," smiled the Lineman cheerily, "do you need fuel, Sir?"

"Yes, mains and auxillaries and check the tire pressures while you're at it, please."

"No problem, Sir."

Jean Paul greeted them when they walked into the FBO.

"Hello, you outlaw," he said smiling.

"Hello, you French Casanova. You know Gutterman and Bender?"

"Yes, how are you, men?" he said extending his hand to them.

"Hello, Jean Paul, long time no see."

"Got anything new on this thing?" asked Bronski.

"Yes, Barbara brought me some tapes just as I was leaving to meet you. We'll go to the shop and I'll translate them for you. Like I told Barb, I wish those damn Arabs wouldn't all talk at once, it would make it easier to translate their gibberish."

Jean Paul turned onto Bourbon St. and just before he got to Bienville he pressed his Geni control. The overhead door to a garage opened and he drove in, pressed the control again and the door closed.

"We can go up these stairs to the second floor. There's a covered walkway that will take us to the rear of the shop without being seen."

Gutterman and Bender were amazed at the radio and electronic gear he had in the room. They were twice awed by the speed with which he typed the translation as he listened to the tape.

"You boys have never met Barbara, have you?"

"No, we've heard an awful lot about her though."

"She's a French Mulatto and a real beauty. Smart as a whip and sharp as a tack. Here's photographs of a map and a list of names that she took from one of the rooms. She's working undercover as a maid at the Sheraton where you're staying. She got these while they were down eating. Don't let on you know her if you see her in the hall. By the way, Mona called and said she had rooms for you so you can check in any time.

"I think this map is the location of the buildings they intend to bomb and the list is their intended victims."

Bronski reached for the phone and dialed the office.

"Good afternoon, OSI."

"Hi, Mona, Joe. Will you call Fort Clark duty officer and have him locate Sgts. Ward and Peel? I need them down here right away. Ask if there are anymore dogs at the Fort or nearby, I'll need about two or three more. I'll also need some more men so get hold of Charley and have him round up at least four more. As soon as he gets them and the dogs together have him fly them down. I have the King Air so he'll have to use the Citation."

"OK, are you at Jean Paul's?"

"Yes."

"I'll call you back as soon as I know something. I got you reservations at the Sherarton and I'll call for more when I hear from Charley."

"Thanks, Mona, I'll be waiting for your call."

He turned to the others.

"I'm getting Charley to round up some more men, Sgts. Peel, Ward, Toro, and Raz, and I hope a couple more teams."

"Not to sound stupid, " said Jean Paul, "but who are Toro and Raz?"

Bronski laughed. "They're German Shepherds and are the best sniffers around. They can train them to sniff out just about anything. Ward and Peel are their handlers. They did a great job for me at Fort Rycker when we had that bomb situation and the generals got blown up."

Mona dialed the duty officer at Fort Clark. "Lt. Miller."

"Hello, Max, Mona Ferguson."

His face lit up. "Hello, Mona, how are you?"

"Just fine, Max. Can you locate Sgts. Ward and Peel for me? I need to talk to them."

"Sure thing, Mona, I know just where they are. I'll have one of them call you right away."

"Thank you, Max,"

"For you, Mona, anytine," he smiled.

"CHAPTER FOUR"

Mona located Col. Blake. "Charley, Joe needs about four more men down there right away. I'm waiting for a call from Sgts. Ward and Peel. He wants them down there, too."

"OK, Mona, I'll see who I can round up and call you back."

The phone rang and Mona picked it up.

"Good afternoon, OSI."

"This is Sgt. Peel, Miss Mona."

"Oh, good, Sergeant, Col. Bronski wants you and Sgt. Ward down in New Orleans and he wants to know if there are any more trained dogs like yours at the Fort or nearby?"

"Yes, Miss Mona, there are two more here. How soon does he want us?"

"As soon as you can get ready. Can you get the other two, also?"

"We can be ready in about forty-five minutes."

"Good, Col. Blake is rounding up some more men for the Colonel so I'll have him pick you up. Where would be a good place, at the Operations building?"

"That will be fine, we'll be waiting."

Mona no sooner hung up when Col. Blake called.

"Mona, Charley, I've got four men and I can get more if he needs them. I can't get away just now, but Nelson is going o fly them down."

"That's fine, Sgts. Ward, Peel, and two more dog teams will be at the Operations building. Can you have Howie pick them up?"

"I'll tell him. He's better take the Citation if he has all of them to haul."

"Joe has the King Air so he said you'd have to use the Citation. I've got to call Joe and let him know what you have, and about the dogs. Can they take off in about an hour and a half?"

"They should be able to get off by then."

191

Jean Paul picked up the phone.

"Jean Paul here."

"This is Mona, Jean Paul, is Joe there?"

"Yes, Mona, he's right here."

"Joe, Mona."

"Hi, Joe. Howie is flying four men down to you along with Sgts. Peel, Ward, and two more handlers with their dogs. He'll be flying the Citation and should be there about 1900 hours."

"That's great, Mona, tell him to come to Lakefront and we'll meet them."

"I told him that's where you would be and got them reservations at the Sheraton, too."

"OK, love, thanks and I'll keep in touch."

He turned to the others. "We've got four more men and four dog teams coming. We'll need four rmore cars. Let's grab some coffee and it will be time to meet them, they'll be here at 1900 hours."

Major Howie Nelson picked up Sgts. Ward, Peel, Gerry, Burr, and the four dogs at Operations.

"Hi, Sergeants, I'm Major Nelson."

The sergeants introduced themselves.

"These are Sgts. Toro, Raz, Otto, and Schnell, the best sniffers in the Army, Sir. Don't mind if they seem to be ignoring you, that's the way they've been trained. They see every move you make and hear everything you say. Talk to them but don't try to pet them."

"Col. Bronski told me about the time he was going to pet Toro and you stopped him."

"They're trained not to let anyone touch them but us. That minimizes the chance of anyone harming them."

"That's good, I can understand that. We'll have four more men with us in the plane. They'll meet us at the air strip."

"That's all right, Sir, they're use to riding in cars and planes with other people. As long as we're with them they know it's all right."

Bronski, Gutterman, Bender, and Napier were at the FBO when Nelson called Approach.

"Lakefront Approach, Army 27 Tango."

"27 Tango, go ahead."

"27 Tango, twenty five northeast, landing Lakefront with November."

"27 Tango squawk 0412, say type aircraft."

"Roger, 27 Tango, Cessna Citation, squawking 0412."

"27 Tango, radar contact, enter right down wind for 18 Right, slow to 200 knots in pattern."

"27 Tango roger, 18 Right, 200 knots."

Nelson banked right in a wide sweeping turn for his forty five degree entry to the downwind leg.

"27 Tango contact tower on 119.9, good day."

"27 Tango roger, good day. Lakefront tower, 27 Tango with you."

"27 Tango, you're number two, a commander on a two mile final, maintain separation, cleared to land."

"27 Tango, number two, cleared to land."

Nelson greased the big jet onto the runway just past the numbers and reversed the engines to slow it down.

"27 Tango turn left on Charley and contact Ground on point seven off the runway."

Nelson eased onto the taxiway and called ground.

"Lakefront Ground, 27 Tango on Charley to transient."

"27 Tango, cross 18 Left and follow the jeep to parking."

The jeep with the checkered flag met him as he turned onto Alpha and led him to parking. He made a wide turn into the tiedown spot and cut the engines at the signal from the lineman.

Bronski walked up to the plane just as the door opened and the steps slid out. Sgt. Peel stood in the doorway grinning and saluted.

"Hello, Sergeant, glad to see you."

"Hello, Colonel, we've go two more dogs for you."

"Good, I think we're going to need them."

Sgt. Ward emerged, followed by Toro, Raz, and the two other sergeants with their dogs. Peel introduced them.

"These are Sgts. Burr and Gerry, and these are Schnell and Otto, Sir."

The two sergeants saluted, Bronski extended his hand.

"Good to meet you, Sir, we've heard a lot of good things about you."

"I'm glad to meet you, but don't believe everything Sgt. Peel tells you. Just kidding, I think we're going to keep you all busy.

The four agents climbed out of the plane, Lindmark, Butcher, Walls, and Craft.

"Hi, fellas, I hope you didn't try to pet the dogs on the way here."

"Hello, Joe, you don't see any missing fingers, do you?"

They held up their hands laughing. "Great dogs, smart enough to be colonels."

Bronski turned to the sergeants.

"We've got a problem, boys. There are eight terrorists here who are planning to blow up some state and government buildings, and assassinate a long list of government officials."

"I think we can do a job for you, Sir," said Peel.

"I'm sure you will, right, Toro?" The dog looked up at him. Bronski laughed. "He knows what I said. We picked up four more cars for you fellows to use."

Nelson stuck his head out of the door.

"Hello, Joe, if you don't need me for anything more, I'll be heading back. Will you be needing any more men?"

"Yes, see if you can round up about four more. Three if you're available, I'd like you here."

"OK, I'll see what I can do. See you tomorrow."

"Let us get the dogs' rations before you start, Sir," called Peel. He and Ward hauled the cases of rations out of the plane. "I'll get one of the cars, Sir."

"We've got reservations for all of you at the Sheraton. You'll be able to take the dogs in there with you."

At the hotel the bellman started to stop them with the dogs.

"I'm sorry, Sir, but they don't allow pets in the hotel."

"It's all right," said Bronski, "these aren't pets, they're seeing eye dogs, the sergeants are all deaf."

The bellman stammered. "Oh. Oh, I guess they're allowed."

The sergeants almost choked trying to keep from laughing.

Bronski saw to it that there were two sergeants and their dogs to a room.

Peel said to Bronski, laughing, "I'll bet that bellman is still trying to figure that one out."

"Just then there was a knock on the door. Bronski answered it. When he opened it a well-dressed man was standing there.

"Please pardon the intrusion, I am Mr. Peterson, the hotel Concierge. I'm afraid there has been a misunderstanding. Do you have dogs in here?"

"Come in, Mr. Peterson. I am Col. Bronski of the OSI. These gentlemen are Sgts. Peel and Ward. The two dogs that you see are very well trained to locate explosives and other things. They are very valuable property of the Army and cannot be left alone. You must not repeat this to anyone, but we have found out that there are some terrorists in the city who are planning to place explosives in the city hall and several other government buildings The dogs are here to help us locate the explosives before they're set off. The dogs must stay with their handlers. They'll be no trouble, like I say, they're very well trained."

Peel called out to Toro. "Go sit by the door and stay, Toro."

Toro went to the door and sat so no one could get past him.

"He'll stay there until I tell him otherwise. Watch, Toro, come sit by the window and stay."

The dog obeyed. Mr. Peterson nodded his head, apparently impressed.

"Very well, since they're seeing eye dogs for the deaf sergeants, I can see it's necessary for them to be here," He said smiling. "Good night, gentlemen, sorry to have disturbed you. If you have any problems let me know."

Bronski smiled. "Thank you, Mr. Peterson, and good night." he closed the door behind him.

Ward and Peel broke out laughing. Bronski joined them.

"Nice fellow, he got the joke."

The four agents came in and the other sergeants followed them.

"I'm going to see the manager after a while and arrange for you two, Lindmark and Craft, to act as maintenance men. You'll start working on the lights by the elevators on the fourth floor so you can get pictures of these birds. They're in rooms 404, 406, 408, and 410. Butcher and Walls I want you to station yourselves in the lobby. When any of them get in the elevator to go down, Lindmark or Craft will call you on the radio and alert you. If they go out, follow them.

"I've arranged to have two of our cars parked by the front door at all time so use them to tail whoever leaves and keep reporting in. The important thing is to get their pictures."

"CHAPTER FIVE"

That evening Bronski talked to the manager and made arrangements for Lindmark and Craft to work on the lights.

The next morning early they set up two ladders and placed their tool boxes on top. These had a camouflaged camera hidden in the bottom end that began snapping pictures of anyone under the ladder as soon as the lid was raised, then stopped when the lid was closed. Butcher and Walls were stationed in the lobby.

At 0700 all eight men came from their rooms and headed for the elevator. They naturally looked up when they came to the ladders so Lindmark and Craft got some excellent shots of their faces. The cameras were so fast that they got six shots of each face before they moved into the elevator. As soon as the elevator doors closed they called Butcher and Walls. Bronski was monitoring the radio and heard the call.

"Joe, we got some great shots of all eight."

"Great, one of you run the film over to Jean Paul. He can develop them and make some enlargements. The other one stay here and if they come back try for some more pictures."

All eight men went to the coffee shop for breakfast. Butcher and Walls managed to get tables on either side of them so they could hear their conversation. Both of them understood Arabic, which was what the men were speaking thinking that no one would understand what they were saying. They were making plans to place a bomb in City Hall, another in the State Capitol, and try to kidnap the Governor.

Walls nodded to Butcher and then got up, saying to the waiter, loud enough for the eight to hear, that he was going to the washroom and would be back. he went out to the lobby, and finding a secluded spot called Bronski on the radio.

"Joe, we just overheard them saying they were going to place a bomb in the City Hall and another in the State Capitol Building. They're also planning to kidnap the Governor."

"OK, I'll take Peel with Toro, Gutteman, and Bender and head for the City Hall. If any of them leave, follow them. I'll send Butcher and Craft, when he returns, to Baton Rouge with Ward and Raz."

Suddenly the eight men came out of the restaurant and Headed for the garage. Butcher and Walls went for their cars. Two of the terrorists drove out and they each followed one. Walls called Joe on the radio and told him what had happened.

"Neither one seems to be heading in the direction of the City Hall, Joe, but we'll stay on their tails."

Craft hurried to Jean Paul's with the film. There was no one in the store except the clerk who was actually an employee of the OSI. Jean Paul was in the rear. Craft slipped through the curtain and entered the rear room. Jean Paul took the film and immediately went into his dark room to develop it. Craft followed him.

In record time he developed the film and made several enlargements of each exposure. Each exposure was an individual's face.

Craft rushed them back to the hotel just in time to catch Bronski and Peel leaving for the City Hall.

Bronski had just turned off LaSalle St. onto Perdido when one side of the City Hall building blew out, taking most of the offices on that side, including the Mayor's with it. Bronski stepped on the gas to avoid the shower of bricks that was flying through the air and screeched to a stop in front of the main entrance.

He hollered to Peel to stay by the car with Toro and the

three of them ran for the open doors.

Inside the building, women were screaming and people were peeking out of their doors to see what happened. Bronski saw a man in his shirt sleeves staring out at the empty space where the offices had been.

He ran up to him. "Was anyone in those offices?"

"I don't think so. I had just left my office to see the comptroller and my secretary hadn't come in yet. I don't think there was anyone in the other offices."

"Where's the Mayor's office?"

"It was there, I'm the Mayor."

"I'm Col. Bronski from the OSI. We were on our way here to warn you and see if we could prevent this."

"I'm afraid you're a little late."

"Can we go someplace and talk?"

"We can use this office here."

In the office Bronski picked up the phone.

"Operator, get me the police, quick, this is an emergency."

"Police station, Sgt. O'Dowd."

"This is Col. Bronski, connect me with your Chief and hurry."

"Chief LeBond speaking."

"Chief, this is Col. Bronski of the OSI. Someone just set off a blast in the City Hall. Can you get over here in a hurry with some men? The Mayor's life is in danger and needs your protection."

"I'll be there as soon as I can with a squad."

Bronski broke the connection and started to call the Fire Department, but the sound of sirens stopped him. He had just set the phone down when he saw the fire engines through the window. He turned back to the Mayor.

"Your Honor, we have it from a good source that your name is on a list of government officials that this group of terrorists plan to assassinate."

"You're kidding."

"I wish I were, Sir." he gave the Mayor all the information they had. "I want to go check on my men, Sir, would you stay right here until the police arrive? I'll send one of my men to stay with you. He'll flash his badge when he comes in. I want to be sure you're protected."

Outside Bronski saw that Peel had his forty-five on a man leaning up against a brick pillar. Toro was also guarding him. Bronski rushed up.

"What's this, Peel?"

"This is one of the terrorists, Colonel, I recognized him from the pictures, see that scar on his face?"

"Right, good work, Peel."

Four police cars pulled up just then. Several officers jumped out, including the Chief. He walked over to Bronski and Peel.

"What have we here?"

"I'm Col. Bronski, Chief, this is Sgt. Peel and we're pretty sure this is one of the terrorist, most likely the one that planted the bomb here. Can you have a couple of your men take him to the station and hold him until we get through here?"

"Certainly." He called two of his officers over. "Take this bird in and lock him up. Don't leave him alone until the Colonel gets there."

"I want to go through the wreckage and see if I can find any evidence. I'd appreciate it if your men would keep the curious away."

"Sure thing, Colonel." He turned and issued orders to his men.

"The Mayor is in one of those side rooms with one of my men. You'd better assign a couple of your men to guard him until we catch these guys."

"Will do." He called to one of his men. "Harington, take Dowdy and find the Mayor. He's in one of the side rooms with the Colonel's man. Stay with him like a flea on a hound. We're giving him twenty-four hour protection until further notice. Get on it."

"Come on, Peel, let's see what we can find in this mess, bring Toro, maybe he'll sniff out something."

They started through the wreckage, picking up something here and there. Toro would stop occasionally and sniff.

When Bronski looked he would find a piece of evidence and place it in his plastic bag.

After three hours of searching Bronski called to Peel. "Come on, Sergeant, we've covered it pretty well and have enough evidence to tell us what he used and how he set it off. These guys are dangerous, they know what they're doing. Looks like a repeat of "Operation Boom" at Fort Rycker. Let's go over to the police station and see what we can get out of this bird."

Gutterman and Bender met them at the car.

"I think we've found this guy's car, it's a Hertz rental and sitting over there. We called the rental agency and they confirmed that it was one of theirs and that an Arab had rented it for an unspecified time. They have three more. He gave us the license plate numbers and description of them."

"Good work, we'll be able to put out an APB if we have to start looking fro them. We're going over to the police station to question him. If he has the keys we can take it back to Hertz."

"Too bad Mac and Boone aren't here to help question him."

"We may wind up getting them," laughed Bronski.

Bronski and the others walked into the police station and inquired about their prisoner.

"I'm Col. Bronski, where have you got the prisoner they brought in from the City Hall?"

"You got here just in time, Colonel, we were just getting ready to go back and beat the hell out of him to shut him up. He's been screaming something in a foreign language ever since they brought him in."

They took him back to the holding cell. The prisoner was one of the Libyans and was screaming in Arabic.

Bronski walked into the cell and grabbed him by the shirt front.

"You speak English, so knock it off. I can understand Arabic so don't get cute."

The prisoner became indignant.

"I am a Libyan citizen and I must insist that you call the Libyan Consul immediately."

"We aren't going to call anyone. We're going to take your finger prints and if I find just one small portion of your prints on what we found at the explosion I'm going to hang you up by your thumbs, savvy?" Bronski turned to the guard.

"Let's take him to get his prints."

"I had nothing to do with that explosion. I don't know what you're talking about."

"Isn't that funny, that's the first thing a guilty person says. We have your picture that was taken at the hotel with your conspirators and your voice on tape. My men also heard you and your gang planning to put the bomb in the City Hall so all we have to do is match it up and tie you in with the rest of them."

He struggled but the big guard grabbed him by the neck and they got a set of his prints."

"OK," said Bronski, "throw him back in the cell and we'll check this stuff out for his prints."

The Libyan began screaming again.

"Shut up you," growled the guard, "or I'll rap you over the head with this night stick."

Bronski opened the plastic bag and carefully took out several pieces of metal and plastic.

"These are parts of the detonator. I was looking for one of those little discs like we found at Rycker, but I think this was set off by remote control. I wonder where he ditched it? Do you think Toro could find it around the building someplace?"

"We can give him another sniff of that guy then take him back to the hall and check it out. If it's there, he'll find it."

"First let's see what we find out from these pieces."

From the small pieces Bronski lifted off several portions of a print. Placing these under a microscope showed that they were definitely those of the Libyan. Bronski called the department finger print expert to have him make a comparison for a positive identification.

"Definitely those of the same finger, you've got your man," he told Bronski. "I'll make an official report so you can have it for your evidence."

Bronski turned to Peel and the others.

"Take Toro back to the City Hall and see if you can find the remote then come back for me."

Bronski went back to the cell.

"Looks like you're the one that handled the detonator for the explosives, you put your finger prints all over it. Did you think the explosion would make them disappear? Now I have a few questions for you."

"I don't answer questions unless I have a lawyer and the consul here."

"Don't make me laugh, you don't get a lawyer and we don't call the consul until we get some answers."

Silence----------------

"OK, I'm going to let you stew in here for awhile, I'll get back to you later."

On the way out Bronski stopped at the desk.

"If anyone should ask if he's here, tell them I took him with me. Just leave him in there and don't let anyone talk to him. If he hollers ignore him. We'll be back later, we still have seven more of these rats to trap."

"OK, Colonel, if he gets too noisy we'll give him a hickory sleeping pill."

When Bronski stepped outside his radio came to life.

"Joe, Gutterman, we're on our way back to the station. Toro found the missing piece, over."

"Great, bring it on in, over and out."

A few minutes later the car pulled up. The three men and the dog got out.

"Here it is, Joe," said Gutterman, handing him a plastic bag containing the missing remote unit. "Ten to one his prints are all over it."

"Let's take it inside and check."

In the lab, Bronski and the police technician came up with a perfect match.

"I'd say this guy doesn't have any smarts to leaves his prints on everything," said the lab man.

"They never do," said Bronski, "thanks for your help."

Just as they were entering the car, Craft's voice came over the radio.

"Joe, this is Craft. We caught a couple of rats and found their block of cheese. We're on our way back and will meet you at the hotel, over."

"We're at the police station. Why don't you come here, we have another one., over."

"Will do, out."

"Bronski, out."

Less than an hour later, Craft and Lindmark pulled up to the station. They got out and dragged their captives out by their collars. Ward and Raz followed them.

"Take them inside and we'll find a cage for them, then you can tell us all about it."

They locked them all in separate cells so they couldn't talk to each other. On their way out Bronski told the desk sergeant, "Same instructions for those two."

"Right, Colonel."

When they were outside, Craft and Lindmark proceeded to tell what happened in Baton Rouge.

"Those two look like Iraqis," said Bronski.

"Yeah, that's what they said they were and kept hollering about immunity. We got to the Capitol Building just in time. Raz found the explosive right away. We disarmed the detonator then concealed ourselves and waited to see if they would come back to see why it didn't blow. We waited about twenty minutes and these two showed up. Before they could rearm the detonator, Raz jumped one and Ward tackled the other one. We had cuffs on them before they knew what happened. We'd better put a tail on the others, they might decide to take a powder when these three don't show up."

"Good thinking, let's head back to the hotel. I'd better call Walls and see what's happening." He took out his radio. "Bronski to Walls, come in, over."

"This is Walls, Joe, we're tailing these two. Butcher called me a minute ago and it looks like they're heading back to the hotel. I think they're trying to play it cute with a diversion. I don't think they know they're being followed, just running a bluff in case. I heard you say you caught one at the City Hall. We're following them back to the hotel If they do anything different I'll get back to you, over."

"Good, we'll meet you back in the room, over and out."

205

When they were back in the room Bronski called Barbara on the radio.

"Barbara, Joe, can you meet us in our room right away? over."

"I'm on my way, Joe."

In a few minutes she knocked on the door.

"Come in, Barb. Have you got anything on your tapes?"

"Yes, three of them have been in room 404 for the past few hours and I have been recording their conversation. I couldn't understand enough to know what they're up to , but it sounds to me like they're planning something."

"Why don't you replace the tapes and bring them up here? We'll run them over to Jean Paul."

"OK, but why don't I run them over and I'll be right back?"

"All right, in the meantime let's look at the picture she took of the map?" He laid it out on the table. "It looks like they might be getting ready to go ahead with their plans, Let's see what they've marked. They've got Montgomery, Alabama; Atlanta, Georgia; Columbia, South Carolina; Raleigh, North Carolina; Richmond, Virginia; and Washington, D.C. circled on the map. Craft, you take Peel and Toro and head for Montgomery, Lindmark, you take Ward and Raz and head for Atlanta. Walls , you take Burr and Schnell and go to Columbia, and Butcher, you take Ger and Otto to Raleigh."

The phone rang. Gutterman picked it up.

"Yes?"

"This is Nelson, we're at the airport and I have four more men for you."

"Hey, great, just a second." He called to Bronski. "Joe, it's Howie, he's at the airport and has four more men for us."

"Let me talk to him." He took the phone. "Hi, Howie, listen, stay there and we'll be there in a little bit."

"OK, Joe, we'll be in the coffee shop or the FBO."

"All right, we'll be there in a little while." He hung up. "This is good but we'll change our plans."

206

He hung up and said to the others, "We'll keep two of the cars to get you fellows to the airport then take the others back to Hertz and pick up a van. Nelson will fly you to your assigned cities and drop off another man with you. This will save a lot of driving and you can pick up a car when you get there. Gutterman and Bender, you'll come with me and we'll fly our playmates over to Rycker for questioning. We'll need the van to get us to the airport."

"When you get where you're going, contact the local police for backup and to protect the Governor. As soon as Nelson has you all delivered he'll come back to Montgomery to give you a hand, Craft. If you should get lucky and catch these guys, fine, if not and they get away they'll probably head for Atlanta. Nelson can fly you there and you can join up with Lindmark again. We'll catch up to you as soon as we can get away. Any questions?"

"No, we know what to do."

"Good, as soon as we get the translation back we can see what it says and take it fom there."

Barbara knocked on the door and walked in.

"Here you are, Joe, you'd better read this.

The translated conversation told them that the five remaining terrorists were wondering where the three that were captured were.

"They must have been picked up," one of them said, "we can't take a chance and wait for them, they'e expendable, we have to continue without them. We must accomplish our mission before our brethern are sentenced and executed. We will give them another six hours, then leave. They know our plans and if they are free they can catch up to us."

"They smell a rat," said Bronski, "this changes our plans a little. Craft, you go out to the airport and meet Nelson then adfvise him of our plans, you'll take one of the men he brought with him and come back here. Lindmark, you will do the same. You'll all wait here for our friends to leave, then you can follow them. That will make six of you and the dogs to take care of the situation if they all go to

Montgomery. Each of you take a car so you can tail them because if they split up it will most likely be in two groups. Keep Mona informed as to what you're doing and check with her for information. OK, Craft, Lindmark, get going. We'll wait here for you. You can brief Nelson and tell him to wait in Atlanta for me."

Bronski, Gutterman, and Bender picked up the prisoners and took them to the airport to load in the King Air. One of them voiced an objection.

"We do not fly in small planes."

Bronski grabbed him by the arm and shoved him towards the plane.

"You have a choice, you can climb in under your own power or we can carry you in unconsious, which is it going to be?" He drew back his fist threateningly.

The man looked at him and shrugged his shoulders, then climbed into the plane with difficulty, his hands being chained to his waist chain. Once they were in, Gutterman and Bender fastened their chains to the seats.

Less than an hour later Bronski was calling the air strip at Fort Rycker. He had called Gen. Harris from the hotel for permission to bring the prisoners there for questioning. Gen. Bret Hart met them as they taxied into the parking tarmac behind the "Follow Me" jeep. Four MP's were there to transport the prisoners to the stockade.

The jeep swung around and stopped in front of the tiedown space. The lineman jumped our and directed the plane in.

Bronski expertly swung the big plane into the space, stopping the nosewheel on the yellow line marking the center. The lineman drew his finger across his throat signaling Bronski to shut down his engines.

When the props stopped turning, Hart walked around the left wing to the door, followed by the four MP's. Gutterman emerged first and assisted the prisoners, with their waist chains and cuffs, down the steps. The MP's quickly ushered them to the cars and none too gently pushed them into the rear seat, which was separated from the front by an expanded metal screen.

Gutterman extended his hand.

"Hello, Bret. I see no one has put a bomb in your car yet."

"That's because no on wants my job," he returned the humor, laughing. "How've you been?"

"Top notch."

Bender and Bronski emerged from the plane. Hart put out his hand to Bender.

"Hello, Bender, good to see you," he said as they shook hands.

"Hello, Bret. How's that pretty little sergeant of yours, Carol? That's all Joe talks about, I think that's the real reason we're here," he said with a laugh.

Bronski was right behind him. "Hello, Bret, I didn't think I was being so obvious about it," he smiled.

"Hello, Joe. As soon as you get your cargo stored I'll call Carol to come have dinner with us at the "O Club"."

"That would make him happy," laughed Bender.

Bronski walked over to the MP's.

"Take them over and stuff them in the stockade, we'll be along later."

The MP's saluted. "Yes, Sir."

He turned back to Hart. "Did I hear you say you were going to buy the steaks?"

"I could be talked into it. Did you bring Mona?"

"Doggone it, I knew I forgot something," he laughed, "you see fellas, I told you he was a nice guy even if they did make him a general."

"CHAPTER SEVEN"

Col. Hansen met them at Security.

"Hello, Colonel, what have we got here?" he asked as the Mp's herded the prisoners in.

"Hello, Col. Hansen. We've got some boys that like to play with explosives."

"Not again, which one of the generals are they after this time?"

"They're not after generals," laughed Bronski, "they're tying to blow up government buildings and assassinate government officials. It seems that some of their comrades are in the pokey someplace and these birds are trying to pull some terrorist crap to get them released. So far they haven't killed anyone but one of them did manage to blow part of the New Orleans City Hall away. Fortunately no one was hurt. We've got these three but there are five more on the loose that our boys are tailing with Peel, Ward, and a couple more sergeants and their dogs. Have Mac and Pat been here yet?"

"They stopped by and said they would be here when you were ready for them."

"OK, we're going to get something to eat and be back in about an hour.

When they got back to Security Mac and Boone were waiting for them. They both grinned when they saw Bronski.

"Hello, Colonel," hey chorused., "we're ready when you are."

"Hello, boys, thanks for coming. Let me tell you what they're up to," He gave them the story.

"Just the kind we like, Colonel, bring them in."

They brought in the three prisoners. Mac and Boone grabbed the Lybian and slammed him into the chair. Boone held him while Mac drove the nails into the table and tied his hand down. He struggled and began to perspire nervously.

"Why are you doing this thing?" he demanded.

Mac tied his wrist tight.

"That's so you won't bleed to death when I cut off your fingers one at a time."

His eyes grew wide and he struggled with Boone. Mac placed a wad of cotton on the table and drew his knife from the sheath on his belt.

"Are you crazy? You can't do this," he cried, a little frantic.

"Go ahead, Colonel, ask your questions."

"OK, let's start with your name?"

Silence-----------------

Mac took off the first joint of his thumb. He screamed in terror and began yelling in Arabic. The other two looked on in disbelief.

"What's your name?" Bronski repeated.

He babbled something in Arabic. Mac took off the next joint of his thumb. He screamed and struggled to get free.

"Allah! Allah! Protect me from these madmen!"

"Just answer the questions and you won't need Allah. or your comrades," sneered Mac and he raised the knife again.

"No! No! No! It's Youssef Hassan," he sobbed.

"We have a picture of your map where you circled all the State Capitols. Are they where you intend to place bombs?"

He mumbled in Arabic again and Mac took off the first joint of his index finger.

"No, no, please, wait, wait," he sobbed.

"When are they planning to place the bomb in the Capitol Building in Montgomery, Alabama?"

"Tomorrow."

Bronski turned to Gutterman and Bender. "One of you get on the radio and try to contact Craft or Lindmark. Tell them what we learned and to search the Capitol building with the dogs and try to stop them."

"I'll do it," volunteered Bender.

"Go over to Communications, they have a strong enough transmitted o reach them. All right, Hassan, what's next on your agenda?"

"They are going to kidnap the Governor then go to Atlanta."

"Gutterman, go tell Bender to tell them that, too. What happens in Atlanta?"

He hesitated and Mac took off the next joint of his index finger,

He screamed, "Stop, please, I will tell you," he sobbed, "the same thing in Atlanta. They will place the bomb and kidnap the Governor. When they have three or four they will issue a warning, if our comrades are not released they will kill one of the governors until their demands are met."

Bender returned. "I got hold of Craft. All five have left their room. He and Lindmark are tailing them, they'll keep in touch."

"Good." He turned back to the prisoner. Tell me about he counterfeit money you intend to ship in here. When is it due to arrive and how is it being shipped?"

"I don't know about the counterfeit money, the Iraqis are handling that."

Mac raised the knife.

"No, no, they do." He nodded at the two Iraqis.

"Bring one of them over here and put him in the chair. Mac, let this one up and bandage his hand."

They dragged the struggling Iraqi to the table. He broke down and began to sob.

"OK, so tell us."

"It is coming in with four shipments of drugs." He gave them the date of the shipments. He pointed to his companion. "He knows who is going to receive the shipments and arrange for the distribution."

Bronski looked at the other one. "Are you going to give us the information?"

He spat on the floor and cursed Bronski in Arabic. Bronski hit him in the mouth.

"I told you I speak your language," he told him in Arabic. In English he said to Mac, "Put him in the chair and tie him down, I have to get to a phone."

In Hansen's office he dialed the OSI office.

"Good afternoon, OSI."

"Joe, Mona, did you get hold of Conley at the Treasury Dept?"

"Yes, Joe, he's staying at the Marriott in room 212."

"Thanks, Mona, I'll get back to you. Right now I'm in a big hurry."

"OK, Joe, call if you need anything else."

"I will." He broke the connection and dialed the Marriott Hotel in New Orleans."

"Good afternoon, Marriott, may I help you?"

"Hello, this is Col. Bronski, will you connect me with room 212?"

"Hello."

"Conley, this is Bronski, I have some information for you about the counterfeit money."

"Great, Joe, what is it?"

Bronski told him what he had learned.

"Do you want me to call the Coast Guard or the DEA, or would you rather do that? You'll have to coordinate with them."

"I'll call them, Joe, right away."

"All right, we may get some more information, and if we do I'll get back to you. If you don't hear from me, call Mona, I'll keep her informed."

"OK, Joe, and thanks."

Bronski's radio came to life. "Craft calling Bronski, over."

"Bronski here, go ahead."

"They're in three cars, Joe, and it looks like one of them is headed up I55 for Jackson. Lindmark is tailing him. The other two we think are heading for Montgomery. When we're sure, we'll try to get ahead of them so we can get to the Capitol Building first with the dogs.

"Stay with them and keep me posted. We're still at

Rycker questioning these three. I'll let you know if we learn anything I think you can use."

"OK, Joe, over and out."

"Bronski out."

Conley immediately contacted the Coast Guard at Pensacola, St. Petersburg, Miami Beach, Cape Sable, and Fort Lauderdale to cover the proposed landing areas the smugglers were supposed to use. He then contacted the DEA to coordinate with the Coast Guard. Two fast cutters were dispatched to each location.

The smugglers were suppose to make their drop at midnight. The plane was to drop the waterproof containers three miles from shore. They would contain cocaine and counterfeit money. Cabin cruisers were to pick them up and haul them in close to shore where air boats would retrieve them when they were sure it was clear.

The two cutters sat out about two miles from shore, keeping the cruisers on radar. When they saw the cruisers pick up the containers they closed in from two sides, blocking their escape.

The Coast Guard was successful at Cape Coral, Cape Sable, and Miami Beach, but at the islands near the bayous, the cruisers managed to get in among the islands where the cutters couldn't go and escaped in the dark.

Two helicopters were standing by to be notified if the drop was near the islands. They took off as soon as they were called and spotted the air boats.

Automatic rifle fire from one of the boats caused one of the choppers to make a forced landing and the other one lost the boat in the dark.

The captured containers each held packages of counterfeit twenty dollar bills amounting to thirty million dollars plus fifty kilos of raw cocaine.

Conley's expertise enabled him to quickly discover the discrepancy in the phony bills so he could put out the word how to detect them. He immediately contacted every bank in the southeast to be on the lookout for the bills.

"CHAPTER EIGHT"

At Fort Rycker Boone held the Iraqi while Mac tied his wrist and hand to the nails. He struggled and cursed but they held him.

"What's your name?" asked Bronski.

Silence------------------

Mac's knife took off the first joint of his thumb. He screamed again and fear came into his eyes.

Silence------------------

The knife came down again and severed his index finger.

"Aiee! No! No! No! I am Hammed Ali."

"Who is to receive the money and the drugs?"

He kept screaming but didn't answer.

Mac decided to try a bluff. He placed the blade of the knife on the wrist and slowly raised the knife as though he was aiming to take off the hand,.

The Iraqi screamed, "Allah, Allah, save me from these sadists!"

"Talk," snarled Mac.

Between sobs he gave Bronski the names and locations of several contacts. Bronski hurried to the phone and dialed the Marriott again.

"I'm sorry, but Mr. Conley's room doesn't answer the phone."

Bronski thanked her, broke the connection, then dialed his office.

"Good afternoon, OSI."

"Joe here, Mona, I have some vital information for Conley, but he's gone out. Will you try to run him down through the DEA and the Coast Guard and give it to him?" He gave her the information.

"I think we've gotten all the information we can out of these three. We'll leave them in the stockade here then try to catch up with the rest of our boys."

"OK, Joe, " aid Mona, "I'll get right on it. Be careful."

"Thanks, sweetie, I will." He hung up and turned to Gen. Hart. "We'll leave those three here n the stockade. Can you get the Doc over here to look at those hands?"

"Sure, Joe, I'll take care of it." He reached for the phone and called the hospital. "Doc Hill will take care of them."

"Thanks, Bret, we've got to take off now and catch up with the rest of our men."

"As soon as I can get Doc on the line," said Bret, still holding the phone, "we'll run you out to the air strip."

Twenty minutes later, Lind pulled up to the King Air.

"We'll keep those guys cooling their heels until we hear from you, Joe. No one will know they're here."

"Thanks again, Bret. Hopefully it won't be too long." He smiled, "If you want to know what's happening, call Mona."

Bret grinned. "Good idea, I'll keep checking with her."

"Thanks, Bret, for everything, I'll be seeing you, soon I hope."

"If you ever decide you want a star on that shoulder, we've got a place for you here."

"I kind of like this job and the eagles suit me fine."

"Keep it in mind in case you want to take it a little easier."

Bronski snapped him a salute as he climbed in the plane. Hart smiled and returned it. Bronski's salute was his way of showing Hart how highly he regarded him. Hart smiled, he knew this.

"You take it, Gutterman, I'd like to relax and think for awhile."

Gutterman eased the big aircraft up to the runway and called control.

"Rycker Control, Army 35 Bravo ready for take off."

"Army 35 Bravo cleared for take off, no reported traffic."

"35 Bravo roger, rolling."

Gutterman dipped his wing when he saw Hart waving. He climbed to altitude and headed for Montgomery.

"Bender," said Bronski, "give someone a call and see what's going on."

He reached for the mic. "Calling Craft or Lindmark, over."

"This is Craft, over."

"Joe wants to know what's happening and where you are?"

"We're in Montgomery. We went directly to the State Capitol Building and waited. No one showed. Peel and Toro stayed there while we went to the City Hall to check it out. Just before we got there a blast went off and wrecked one wing of the building. Fortunately only two women were hurt and not seriously. We found out they had snatched Governor Folsom. We found their cars nearby and have the local police watching them. I think they dumped them for some different vehicles. We checked with Hertz, Avis, and some other rentals but they haven't rented any cars from them, over."

"Are there any car dealers near there? over.

"Yes, I think there's a couple just down the street, over."

"Check with them and see if they've bought any. They seem to have plenty of cash. It might be counterfeit, too. over."

"OK, where are you now? over."

"We're in the air and should be landing at Maxwell in about a half hour. over."

"Alright, we'll call you as soon as we find out anything, over and out."

"Standing by." He turned to Bronski. "I'll try to raise Lindmark. Bender calling Lindmark. over."

"Lindmark here, go ahead. over."

"What's going on with you? over."

"My man gave me the slip as soon as we got into Jackson so I went directly to the Capitol Building and sent Ward and Raz to the City Hall. No one showed so I put in a call to the City and State Police and gave them a description of the car and the license number with instructions to call me if they spotted it.

"MHP called, they have a tail on it. He's heading east on I80. They're going to try and detain him without making him suspicious, until we can catch up to him. I'll call you

217

as soon as we make contact again. These guys aren't dummies, I think this was a diversion., over and out."

"Bender standing by." He turned back to Bronski. "These things aren't just happening, Joe, I think they've got this all planned out. They've got something else in mind other than just bombing the Capitols."

"I think you're right, maybe that's a cover and they're going to attempt the assassinations. We'd better check to see if they've made any demands yet."

"We'd also better make sure they've got some protection for that list of officials you gave to the SS agent."

The radio came to life. "Craft calling Bender, over."

"Bender here, go ahead, over."

"You guessed it, they bought three cars, Cadys, one black, one blue, and one green. That's not all, they've snatched Governor Folsom. We've got an APB out to the AHP, GHP, and all law enforcement agencies east of here, over."

"We'll keep in contact with you, over and out."

"CHAPTER NINE"

The MHP that was tailing the terrorist lost him in Newton. His car was finally located in a supermarket parking lot but no sign of him. They searched the town for about an hour when word came that a car had been stolen in the same parking lot.

Radioing ahead they set up a road block at Meridian, assuming that he was trying to meet up with his comrades in Montgomery. They also had the local radio stations broadcast his description over the air. A call came from a Billy Watson.

"I think I saw the man you're looking for."

"Where, when?"

"About an hour ago. I'm the lineboy at the Meridian Airport. He came n here and chartered a plane from Mr. Daly. They took off right away."

"Did they say where they were going?"

"No, but there's a copy of his flight plan here. Hold on, I'll get it." He was back in a few minutes. "Here it is. He has Biloxi as his destination but when he took off he headed straight east"

"Good work, son. What kind of plane was it and the tail number?"

"It's a red and white twin Comanche, tail number 6025P."

"All right, son, good work. If you ever need a favor, look me up, I'm Sgt. Callahan of the State Police."

"Thanks, Sergeant, I'll remember. I guess you know enough to call the FAA and see if they have him on radar."

"Yes, thanks, I will."

Sgt. Callahan called the FAA.

"This is Sgt. Callahan, MHP. We're looking for a red and white twin Comanche, tail number 6025P, destination Biloxi, can you help us?"

"We had two plane headed for Biloxi. One has arrived but the other one canceled his flight plan just north of

Natchez. Let's see, yes, here it is, twin Comanche 6025P. They dropped off radar just after that. We'll check the airports in the area if you'd like."

"We'd appreciate it. Contact HQ if you find anything."

"Lindmark to Bronski, over."

"Go ahead, over."

"We've lost our pigeon. He switched cars then chartered a plane in Meridan. The pilot filed for Biloxi but cancelled his flight plan just north of Natchez and disappeared off radar. He's probably going to Atlanta to meet his partners. I'm going to charter a plane for us and we'll meet you in Atlanta, over and out."

"Call me when you get there, over and out."

Lindmark found a pilot with a Beech Baron. He was a little reluctant about having Raz in the plane, but Ward assured him there was nothing to worry about that Raz had flown many times.

"Bronski calling Craft, over."

"Go ahead, Joe, over."

"We're at Maxwell getting ready to take off. Lindmark chartered a plane and is going to Atlanta. We'll meet you there, Over."

"OK, Joe, these three have left town, I'm sure. I've got the local police watching the City Hall and the Capitol Building, over."

"Fine, keep in contact, over and out."

"Will do, over and out." He turned to Peel. "Hold onto your hat, I'm going to see just how fast this Chrysler Imperial will go. We'll probably have every HP between here and Atlanta on our tail."

Peel grinned. "Let 'er rip, Sir."

Gutterman dropped their flight plan off at Operations and boarded the plane. Bender was going to fly.

"We sure like it when you're on a case, Colonel, gives us a chance to get away from the Fort," smiled Mac.

Bronski smiled. "I'm glad I'm on the good side of the Old Man. He said I could have you anytime I wanted. We couldn't get near the information we do without you two."

"They grinned. "Trouble is, Colonel, we're beginning to like this kind of work."

They all laughed.

"Fifty two minutes later, Bender was calling Atlanta Halsfield International Approach on 119.3.

"Halsfield Approach this is Army 35 Bravo, 25 southwest landing, we have Romeo."

"35 Bravo squawk 0425. make straight in for 02 Left. Altimeter 30.25, wind calm. Contact tower on 120.9 ten miles out."

"Army 35 roger."

Ten miles out Bender called the tower.

"Halsfield Tower Army 35 ten out."

"35 Bravo cleared to land 02 Left."

Bender touched down just past the numbers.

"35 Bravo, where do you park?"

"We're transient."

"If able make the next taxiway and contact Ground on point nine."

"35 Bravo roger." He made the next turn. "Halsfield Ground 35 Bravo off the runway to transient parking."

"35 Bravo follow the "Follow Me" at the intersection."

"35 Bravo roger."

The Jeep led them to parking and indicated a tiedown spot. Bender swung the big plane and stopped. The lineman drew his finger across his throat to cut the engines. The lineman chocked the wheels and fastened the tiedown ropes while they were exiting.

"Hey, Joe, look, there's our Citation."

27 Tango was in the next tiedown space.

"That means Nelson is here, try to raise him on the radio."

Gutterman keyed the mic. "Nelson, this is Gutterman, come in, over."

"Stop hollering, I'm right here in the FBO," laughed Nelson.

He greeted them when they walked in the office.

"Hello, Howie, what's happening?"

"I heard most of your conversation on the radio and figured you'd need me here. I sent the four that I brought with me to Washington to make sure that the President and Vice-president are well guarded. I dropped Walls, Burr, and the dog off in Columbia, S.C. and kept Butcher, Gerry, and the dog with me in case you needed them. They're out in the car I rented."

"That's good, here's the situation as it stands now." He brought Nelson up to date. "Send Butcher, Gerry, and the dog to the City Hall to check and guard the Mayor. Bender you better take Mac and Boone to the Capitol Building, and the rest of us will go see the Governor."

They started out the door and a police car drove up with an officer and a sergeant in it. The sergeant got out.

"I'm looking for Col. Bronski, is that you, Sir?"

"I'm Bronski, Sergeant."

"Sgt. Wilks of the Atlanta Police. Are you looking for a twin Comanche, tail number 6025P?"

"Yes, we are."

"Well, we've found it at South Fulton Airport, about fifteen minutes southwest of here."

"What about the men in it?"

"There was only one man in it, the pilot, he was in the rear seat, dead."

"Damn, I wonder where that SOB is now?" The sergeant looked puzzled. "I mean the guy he was flying, he's the one we want." Bronski opened his attache case

222

and took out the pictures of the five terrorists that were still on the loose. "He's one of these. The others are on their way here from Montgomery."

"Give me a set of those pictures, Sir. I'll get copies made and spread them around. If he's in the city, we'll find him."

"I'd like to set up road block on every road leading into the city."

"I can do that for you, Sir. Let me get on the radio and get the ball rolling."

"Good, they should be getting here soon. Let's see if we can get couple of choppers in the air and maybe they can spot them. I don't think they'll come in on I85, they'll probably use a side road. Gutterman, Bender, get over to the Helicopter service and each of you go up in one."

"Gutterman calling Bronski, over" (In the chopper)
"Bronski here, go ahead, over."
"OK, Joe, we're skirting I85 about fifteen miles out. We should be able to spot them easy, over."
"Good, where's Bender? Over."
"Bender here, Joe, we're covering I20, over."

"Joe, Gutterman, we've spotted the blue and black Cadys. I'm sure it's them, they're traveling close together. The green one must have turned off some place or is lagging way behind. We've dropped down behind them and can read the license plates, that's them. They're turning on the off ramp 15 and are heading north on 285. Better get some cars to cover the side roads. Bender, can you get your pilot to search for that green Cady? Over."

"We're on our way, over."
Bronski keyed his mic. "We have four cars, I'm with the Sergeant and his driver. We're heading up to block the side roads, if they turn off we've got them."
"Joe, they've turned off on Washington Road and are heading northeast."
"We're on Herschel, we can cut them off. All right,

"Sergeant, let's set up a road block at the intersection. Gutterman, we're almost at the intersection, where are they?"

"They're about two miles away yet, Joe."

"OK, we're setting up a road block. I'm sending a couple of cars that way to prevent them from turning back."

"Joe, I think they've spotted your road block and are attempting to turn around. The cruisers are trying to block them."

"We're heading that way."

"They have the black one stopped but the blue one is getting away."

"We see him, driver, step on it."

Two patrol cars had the black Cady stopped when Bronski in another car sped past them in pursuit of the blue one.

"You're pulling up on him, Joe," called Gutterman.

"We're on him , but it doesn't look like he's going to stop. Let's try to run him off the road."

"There's no traffic coming towards you, Joe."

"OK, driver, pull alongside him and we'll see if we can make force him to stop."

They pulled alongside and Bronski signaled him to stop. Instead he pulled out a gun and without looking fired a shot at them. The slug hit the door frame.

The Sergeant puled his gun and fired back, causing the terrorist to swerve a little. He turned his gun and fired at the rear tire, hitting it. The Cady began to swerve back and forth, gaining momentum.

Finally the driver lost control and went off the road, flipping over and rolling down the embankment. Joe was out of the patrol car before it stopped and ran back to the crash, followed by the two policemen. The driver was crushed and pinned under the steering wheel

Bronski and the officers tried to free him, but he gave them a blank stare, coughed up blood, and took him last breath.

"Well," said Bronski, "that takes care of him. I wonder what they did with the Governor?"

"He's not in the car, let's see if we can get the trunk open and check it. Get the keys out of there, Delaney," said the Sergeant.

They unlocked the trunk and it fell open. It was empty, but a fountain pen fell out on the ground. Bronski bent over to retrieve it. It was an expensive Waterman Laureat Gold fountain pen. The initials J.E.F. were engraved on it.

"This must belong to Gov. Folsom. They probably had him in here and this dropped out of his pocket. They didn't see it when they moved him. He might have left it there on purpose as a clue. I wonder where he is now? Let's go check the other Cady."

The cruiser pulled up.

"You boys stay here until the tow truck and the ambulance comes," ordered the Sergeant.

Mac and Boone were in one of the patrol cars that stopped the black Cady. They had the terrorists leaning against the car with their legs spread.

"Good work, boys. We found Gov. Folsom's pen in the trunk of the other car so let's check this one. The other guy is dead. The Sergeant shot out his tire and he lost control, went off the road, and flipped over."

"Here's the keys," said Boone.

"OK, open it up and let's take a look."

The Governor wasn't there, but a box containing explosives, a container of detonators, and another box with timers were under some blankets.

"Those idiots, they could have blown themselves to hell with those detonators and explosives next to each other like that. Lets get this stuff separated before we get it. We'll take these two over to Fort McPherson and maybe we can find a room to interrogate them."

"I'll have to go back to the plane and get my bag," said Mac.

"Alright, one of the patrol cars can run you back, then meet us at the Fort. We'll put these two in the back of this one. Sergeant can you get a couple of tow trucks to intern this car and scrape up the other one?"

"I've already called them. They should be here in a few minutes with a meat wagon to pick up the body."

"OK, you take care of that and we'll get going with these two."

"Think you can get them to talk?"

"Mac and Boone learned some methods in the Orient that are very effective, they'll talk."

"I'd like to see that," smiled the Sergeant.

"If you have a strong stomach, come along."

"That rough, huh? Yeah, I can stand anything that happens to these kind."

Bender came on the radio.

"Bender calling Bronski, over."

"This is Bronski, go ahead, over."

"We haven't been able to spot the green Cady, Joe, they must have slipped past us somehow. Do you think they're heading for Washington?"

"He must have gotten here ahead of the others and picked up the one from the plane. We've got the other two and are taking them to Fort McPherson for questioning. Go on up the highway and see if you can spot them. We'll put out an APB on them. Call me when you get back."

"Right, Joe, over and out."

Bronski introduced himself to Gen. Laird, the commandant of Fort McPherson.

"A pleasure to meet you, Colonel, your name is familiar to me. How can I be of service to you?"

"We have a couple of terrorists we want to interrogate and need a place with extreme privacy."

"No problem, Colonel" He reached for the intercom and buzzed his aide.

"Yes, General?"

"Harmon, get me Col. Pulaski at Security."

"Yes, Sir, right away."

His phone lit up.

"Col. Pulaski, here, what can I do for you, Sir?"

"Col. Pulaski, I have Col. Bronski here in my office from the Office of Special Investigations. He needs a secure room to interrogate a couple of suspected Terrorists."

"No problem, Sir, send the Colonel over."

"Thank you, Colonel."

He stood up and extended his hand.

"He's a stiff neck, but he'll take care of you. Good luck, Colonel, and give my regards to Gen. Miner when you get back to the office."

"Thank you, Sir, I will."

CHAPTER ELEVEN

"Col. Pulaski, I'm Col. Bronski."

"Glad to know you, Colonel, come with me." He led them back to a room and opened the door. "Here you are, Colonel. it's sound proof."

"This will be fine. One of my men, Sgt. MacMillan, will be arriving shortly, will you direct him back here?"

"Will do."

Twenty minutes later Mac knocked on the door and entered. The two prisoners were sitting at a table facing each other.

"OK, Mac and Boone, whenever you're ready."

Mac sat his bag on the table and began removing the contents. The knife in the sheath he hooked to his belt and then drove two nails in the table and tied a thong to one of them. Boone held on to the prisoner while he tied his wrist then his hand to the table.

"Why are you doing this thing?" he asked, wide eyed.

"So you won't jerk your hand when I cut off your fingers for not answering the Colonel's questions and cause me to miss."

He looked at Mac with contempt in his eyes and snorted, not believing him.

"Ha! You American, you bluff!"

"OK, Colonel. we're ready."

"What's your name?"

He sneered at Bronski, then turned his head and spit.

Mac brought the knife down and took off the first joint of his thumb then jammed a wad of cotton on it.

He looked at his severed thumb in disbelief and then screamed.

"You didn't answer the Colonel's question," said Mac and raised the knife again.

"No! No! I'm Oupra Adit."

"What have you done with Governor Folsom?"

Silence----------------------

Mac slammed the knife down and took off the rest of his thumb.

He screamed again and babbled in Arabic.

"You didn't answer," sneered Mac and he raised the knife again.

"Please, no, he's in the other car."

"Where are they and where are they headed?"

"They are on their way to your Capitol."

"What are they planning to do there?"

Silence-----------------------

Mac took off the end of his index finger.

"No, no, no, in the name of Allah, please stop!" He was practically hanging from the table trying to get free of Boone. The Sergeant helped Boone restrain him. The other prisoner sat there horrified at what he was seeing.

"I stop when you talk," said Mac and he raised the knife threateningly.

"No, please, they re going to assassinate your president if our comrades are not released."

"What about Governor Folsom?"

"They will demand the release of our comrades and if they are refused they will kill the Governor. After that they will kill the President," he sobbed.

"Where do they plan to do this?"

"At the Arlington Cemetery, the President will be there the day after tomorrow for the burial of Gen. Pelan."

"OK, get Pulaski to stick these two in the stockade and hold them incommunicado."

"Jesus Chrrist, Colonel, " said the Sergeant, "when you said your men had ways to make them talk I didn't realize they would be that brutal. You don't screw around, do you?"

"We can't afford to mollycoddle these people, there are lives at stake. Right now it's the President's and Governor Folsom's. Don't you approve?"

"Hell yes, if I thought I could get away with that stuff, I'd sure as hell use it to make some of these birds sing," smiled Sgt. Wilks.

229

"Col. Pulaski, I need to store these prisoners in your stockade and I don't want it known they're here."

"No problem, Colonel, consider it done. I've got a couple of tough sergeants, too."

"Good, I'll be in touch. Right now we have to get to Washington. Can you get a doctor over here? He got his fingers caught in the fan."

"What fan?"

"The ceiling fan."

"Oh? OH, YEAH.," he smiled. "I'll take are of that."

"CHAPTER TWELVE"

Bronski called Gutterman and Bender on the radio.

"Bronski calling Gutterman and Bender, come in, over."

"Gutterman here, Joe, I'm at the airport."

"This is Bender, we're over the city."

"Gutterman, stay where you are. Bender come to the airport, ASAP, over."

"OK, Joe, we'll be there in five, over and out."

Bronski and two patrol cars rolled into the airport and out to the two planes on the tarmac.

"Nelson, load up and head for Washington, pronto." He then briefed all of them on what he had learned. Get as many men as you can out to Arlington and start combing the city for that green Cady. Gutterman, Bender, have your pilots fly you all the way up the highway to Washington and look for it. If you spot it, try to stop it, if not, proceed to Washington. Get some cars and start searching. We'll be right behind you."

Nelson fired up the Citation and took off with Bronski right behind him in the King Air.

Gutterman and Bender took off in the choppers to search I85 to Charlotte, N.C., where they split up. Bender went north following I75 to I81, then I66 to Washington, with no luck.

Gutterman stayed on I85 to Richmond, Va., then I95 to Washington. He had no luck spotting the green Cady either. The earth seemed to have swallowed it up.

Nelson and Bronski landed at Washington Municipal. They had radioed ahead and cars were there waiting for them. Gutterman and Bender arrived later.

Bronski immediately contacted the White House for the Secret Service Agent in charge. He alerted him of the danger that the President would be in if he attended the funeral.

"You know how strong headed the President is, Colonel. We'll just have to be doubly aware because he'll be there regardless."

OK, we're getting every available man we have out there to cover the grounds. I'd suggest you do the same."

Bronski put out an APB on the Cady and the two terrorists, then sent several men to search the area surrounding Arlington Cemetery.

The flag draped caisson carrying the remains of Gen. Rudolph Pelan, followed by the horse with the reversed boots hanging from the saddle, and the uniformed procession, entered Arlington Cemetery.

When the President and the rest of the dignitaries were set, the colorful Army Guard took its position alongside the grave site and the Army Chaplin stepped to the head of the coffin, where it was placed on the lowering device over the grave.

Bronski and several of his men walked around the outside the crowd, searching. His radio came to life. He had the volume turned down so not to disturb the service.

"Gutterman to Bronski, over."

"Go ahead Gutterman, over."

"We've located the Cady at an abandoned warehouse about a mile from the cemetery, over."

"Have you located the suspect yet? Over."

"He's inside the building, we only saw one. He has a gun in his hand and the Governor is tied to a chair. We're checking to see if there's some way we can get in and surprise him. We don't want to put the Governor in jeopardy, over."

"OK, we're looking for the other one here, keep in touch, over and out."

A moment later the Secret Service Agent standing alongside the President let out a yell and fell to the ground. A bullet had hit his upper arm and went through to his shoulder. Quickly the other agents surrounded the President. A woman screamed, "He's been shot!" No sound had been heard.

Bronski and his men quickly looked around.

"He must have a silencer, I think the shot came from the direction of that tree, isn't that a wisp of smoke coming out of those branches?"

They drew their guns and ran towards the tree, firing into the branches as they went. Just as they got there a man tumbled out of the tree, he had been shot in several places.

"Help me," he pleaded.

"Help you!" snapped Bronski, "I ought to blow your head off. Get a car, Brennan, and we'll get him out of here to the prison ward in the hospital."

Two Secret Service men came running up.

"Go take care of the President," said Bronski, "the danger is over, this is the last of them. Sorry about the interruption, give my apologies to the President. We'll take care of this scum."

They loaded him roughly in the car, ignoring his screams of pain, and drove off.

Gutterman called Bronski.

"We've got the Governor, Joe, and we're sending him to the hospital for a check up. The SOB was about to shoot him. Their request for the release of their comrades was turned down, over."

"Did you capture the Iraqi?"

"Yes, but I'm afraid he won't be talking. Our first shot knocked his gun away and the second would have spoiled his aim, it went through his eye. I don't think he wanted to be captured, over."

"Good work, we've got the other one. He needs some medical attention. He damn near hit the President, but hit an agent instead. He's hurt pretty bad, but I think he'll make it. Give me directions to where you are and we'll meet you, over." Gutterman gave him the directions.

The local police were called to take care of the body and impound the Cady. At the hospital the doctor was checking over Gov. Folsom, who wanted to get dressed and be released. The Doctor insisted that he remain for a couple more days for observation, much to the chagrin of the Governor.

"Col. Bronski!" he exclaimed from his hospital bed when Bronski walked in. "I don't know how to thank you for saving my life. Those men intended to kill me."

"No thanks necessary, Governor. Here, I have something you lost." He handed him the Wateman Laureat pen.

The Govenor laughed. "I left it in the trunk of the car hoping they wouldn't see it and to give someone a clue as to where I was. I'm glad you found it."

Bronski told him what happened to the blue Cady.

"It's a good thing they moved you to the other car or you might not have been here to talk about it. The car was really smashed up. Has your family been notified?"

"Yes, I just talked ot my wife and they're flying her up here this evening in Air Force One."

"That's fine, Sir. She should get a thrill out of that. Well, you're in good hands now."

"Have you captured all of those men?"

"Yes, Sir, we have three at Fort Rycker, two at Fort McPherson, two are dead, and one is shot up pretty bad."

"Fine work, Colonel, you and your men are to be commended."

"Just doing what we're trained to do, Sir. I wish you a speedy recovery. I have to leave now. I'm glad we could be of service."

"Thank you again, Colonel, and God bless all of you."

Bronski had no sooner arrived at headquarters when Gen. Miner called him into his office.

"Hello, Joe, what have you been up to? I received a call from the President's office a few minutes before you came in and as many of your men as you can round up have been ordered to be at the White House this evening at 1900 hours."

"Did they say what it was about?"

"No, I guess you're all being called on the carpet."

Bronski got a concerned look on his face.

Miner laughed. "They did say you were to be in Mess Dress Uniforms. I have a hunch he wants to hang a medal on you for saving his and several Governors lives."

Bronski grinned. "In that case I'd better start rounding them up. I'm going to take Mac, Pat, Peel, Ward, Burr, and Gerry with me. They all played a vital part in all this."

"I don't think that will be any problem. You're to be there at 1900 hours for cocktails. Let me know how many there will be as soon as possible."

"I'll get back to you as soon as I know."

He turned and hurried out. When he got to Mona's desk he stopped.

"Dig out your sexiest formal, sugar, we're all invited to the White House for dinner tonight."

Mona was startled. "All of us?"

"Everyone that was involved in cleaning up this case. We're to be there at 1900 hours. We'll meet here."

He gave her some names to call.

"That's great. By the way, Conley called to thank you. They recovered all the counterfeit money and the narcotics. He said to tell you he owes you one."

Bronski got hold of Mac, Pat, and the sergeants.

"Can you fellows get some Mess Dress Uniforms? We're all invited to the White House for dinner tonight and I think the President wants to thank us personally for saving his life and cleaning up this case."

"I think we can, Colonel. We have a couple of buddies at Clark that are 'Tops' and the same size as we are. I'm sure they have Messys. I'll check with them."

"Good, be at HQ at 1630 hours. We'll leave from there."

Bronski rounded up all the men that were involved in the case and at 1845 hours five cars containing Bronski, Mona, the agents, and the sergeants, all decked out in their finest, medals and all, arrived at the White House gate. The Marine Sergeant guard recognized Bronski and saluted.

"Good evening, Sir, They're expecting you and your party, drive right on in."

Byron, the Vice-president's secretary, was all in a dither and greeted them at the door.

"Good evening, Colonel. And Miss Mona, what a pleasant surprise, follow me please." He took them up the stairs that led to the second floor.

The Vice-president greeted them at the door to the reception hall.

"Good evening, Col. Bronski, and may I assume that this is young lady is the fabulous Miss Mona Ferguson?"

"Good evening, Sir, and yes, this is the fabulous Miss Mona Ferguson. Mona, his excellency, the Vice-president."

Mona blushed slightly and gave him one of her most disarming smiled.

"We finally get to meet, Sir, and you're just as dashing as you sound over the phone."

The Vice-president beamed.

"And you're even more beautiful than I imagined you were."

Bronski rolled his eyes.

"Sir, I would like you to meet the rest of the men that were instrumental in wrapping up this case."

"Fine, Colonel, but here comes the President. Why don't you present them to both of us at the same time?"

He hooked Mona's arm in his. "Mr. President, may I present Miss Mona Ferguson, of the OSI?"

"So you're the Mona I've heard so many wonderful things about, I'm charmed."

"Thank you, Sir, I'm honored. I must have a talk with my press agent, I was going to fire him , but I see he's doing a fantastic job."

All three joined together laughing. The President shook Bronski's hand.

"Good to see you again, Colonel, especially after this afternoon."

"Thank you, Sir, and I would like to introduce the rest of the men who played a vital part in capturing the terrorists and saving the life of Gov. Folsom."

"Yes, I talked to James this afternoon. He is extremely impressed with the performance of you and your men."

Bronski signaled his men to form a line and as they passed he introduced them. When Mac and Pat approached, the President and Vice-president looked at the rank on their shoulders and smiled. He had personally approved that rank for them.

"These two men, Mr. President and Mr. Vice-president, are TAD to the OSI. They're stationed at Fort Rycker. They have served with me on the last four cases and have been most valuable at obtaining information during our interrogations."

The President raised his eyebrows and smiled.

"They were both stationed in the Orient and acquired certain knowledge about the methods used by the Orientals."

He smiled. "I don't think I should know the details, should I?"

"No, Sir, just accept the fact that their methods are very effective and have helped us save lives, yours include. This is Sr. Master Sergeant Sandy MacMillan and Sr. Master Sergeant Pat Boone."

The President smiled. "I don't suppose you're the Pat Boone that sings, are you? Gentlemen, I am honored."

"It is we who are honored, Sirs," said Mac as they shook hands.

"These, Sir, are Sergeants, Peel, Ward, Burr, and Gerry. They are stationed at Fort Clark. Each of them is a dog handler. Their dogs are highly trained to find just about anything, especially explosives."

"Ah yes, I seem to remember, they were with you at Fort Rycker some time ago when a couple of my generals were killed in explosions."

"Yes, Sir, that was Sgts. Peel and Ward. Sgts. Burr and Gerry assisted us on this case. I'm sorry we couldn't bring the other half of the teams, you would have been impressed."

"Gentlemen," announced the President, "it has been a real honor to meet all of you. And now I believe Henry is glaring at me for holding up his dinner, shall we go in?"

"Yo dinnah is gonna git cold ifn yo don stop dat han shakin, Suh."

The President threw back his head and laughed.

"OK, Henry, you can start serving now."

"He took Bronski's arm and led the way to the dining room, followed by the Vice-president with Mona's arm hooked in his. Her backless white evening gown was accentuated by her fantastic bosom and figure. Most of the eyes in the room were on her.

Down the table Mac raised his thumb in a salute to Bronski when he caught his eye. Bronski nodded, smiled, and winked.

The wine glasses were filled and the President stood, holding out his glass, suggesting a toast. Everyone rose.

"Gentlemen, to the Office of Special Investigations and the courageous men that make this great nation of ours a safe place to live. To your health."

They all joined in, "Hear! Hear!"

Bronski's raised his glass. "To our Commander in Chief and the United States of America."

Again, "Hear! Hear!"

When dinner was over, the President raised his hand.

"Shall we retire to the reception hall for brandy, Lady and Gentlemen?"

They rose and followed him. He stopped at an elaborately carved table.

"Gentlemen and Lady, if you will all line up, I would like to present each of you with the Presidential Citation Medal for the fine job you have just completed."

A young major, the aide to the President, picked up a tray on which was stacked the boxes of medals. One by one he pinned their medals on them and shook their hands. When he came to Mona, hers was attached to a red, white, and blue ribbon which he placed around her neck and kissed her cheek. He then stepped back.

"Gentlemen and Lady, I salute you and thank you for the people our great nation."

As one they returned the salute. A tear formed in Mona's eye. She dabbed at it with her hanky.

"CHAPTER FOURTEEN"

"Well," smiled Frank Miner, "did you get your butts chewed out?"

Bronski laughed. "No, actually he was quite pleased with us."

"What about your prisoners?"

"We're flying down to Fort Rycker in the morning to deliver Mac and Pat if I can ever get them to quit mooning over Mona, and bring back the three we have there. Nelson, Gutterman, and Bender are going to pick up the two at Fort McPherson. I wonder if Mona would like to go along? There's a young general down there who's itching to see her."

He stopped at Mona's desk. "I'm flying these two Romeos back to Fort Rycker in the morning, would you like to go along?"

Mona smiled. "Thanks, Joe, but no. I have too much work to do here."

"Bret will be disappointed."

"Actually he's coming back with you. He has a thirty day leave coming."

"Ah hah! I figured there was a skunk in the woodpile when you said no so readily."

Mona glared at him , but smiled to herself.

"Don't you have a report or something to fill out?"

Bronski walked away laughing. "OK, love."

Three days later Bronski walked into the office.

"Mona, I've got a moon-eyes general here who's dying to see you."

Mona squealed and jumped up. "Bret!" She threw her arms around his neck and kissed him hard.

"Joe, will you get lost or something?" she snapped, smiiing.

"OK, ok, I can tell when I'm not wanted. Boy, what appreciation."

When Bret finally released her she looked behind him.

Carol Man was leaning against the door jam smiling.

"Carol!" she cried, "I didn't see you come in."

"You couldn't see anything but stars, on his shoulders I mean. Hello Mona, how are you?"

"Just great, but what are you doing here?"

"I figured if my boss could come all this way to see his true love, so could I."

"She flew in the right seat all the way and couldn't keep her hands off of him."

"I thought there was a new gleam in Joe's eyes," laughed Mona. "What's that on your shoulders, Carol?"

"We figured if she was going to fall for an officer, we'd better make her one so they wouldn't be breaking any Army regulations," smiled Bret.

"Wonderful!" cried Mona.

"CHAPTER FIFTEEN"

Gen. Frank Miner had two envelopes laying on his desk, one large 10 X 13 and one small 4 X 9. He opened the larger of the two and removed the folder marked "Operation Foiled Mission". He smiled and read the first page of the report.

"Operation Foiled Mission"

"The case of the eight terrorists, four Iraqis and four Lybians, that were sent here to obtain the release of their comrades, or destroy government buildings and assassinate government officials, including the President, was only partially accomplished.

"The lives of the intended victims were saved, but unfortunately a charter pilot was murdered by one of the terrorists. Two City Halls were damaged, but without the loss of life. Two women were injured, but not seriously. All terrorists have been apprehended or eliminated.

"The survivors are now in a Federal prison awaiting a speedy trial, which is being prepared by the Attorney General's office with a guarantee of an execution for the one that murdered the pilot,Daly, and a very long internment for the others.

"Attempts by the Ambassadors from both Lybia and Iraq to plea for leniency, though only half heartedly, have been futile."

"Gov. James E. Folsom, who was the only kidnap victim, has been returned to his home in Montgomery where he is resting for a short time before resuming the duties of his office as Governor of Alabama.

"A vote of thanks should be given to the organizations and people that rendered us assistance, namely the following:

Mississippi State and Local Police
Louisiana State and Local Police
Alabama State and Local Police
Gen. Harris and his staff at Fort Rycker
Gen. Laird and his staff at Fort McPherson
Sgt. Wilks and the Atlanta Police

"Complete details of the entire operation are enclosed."

End of report.
Signed,

Joseph Bronski, Colonel
Office of Special Investigations
United States Army

JB:cm
Copies to:
The President of the United States
The Vice-president
The Attorney General
Governor James E. Folsom, Montgomery, Alabama

Gen. Miner picked up the second envelope and opened it, then read the contents.

"Why that sneaky son-of-a---!" he exclaimed. "If I'd known what he was up here to steal my staff I'd have made the place off limits to him!" He stuck his head out the door and hollered, "BRONSKI!"

Joe stuck his head out of his office .

"Something wrong, Chief?"

"Come in here!"

Bronski entered the office. Miner held up the contents of the envelope.

"Did you know about this?" he demanded.

"About what, Chief?" he asked innocently.

"You know WHAT! And wipe the lipstick off your face. That damn Hart has asked Mona to marry him. What the hell are we going to do without her?"

"Oh that, Chief. Yeah, I knew it was going to happen. She wouldn't say yes until she found a suitable replacement."

"Oh yeah! And who would that be?"

"Did I hear someone call my name?" asked Carol, sticking her head in the door and smiling.

Bronski laughed. "You know Lt. Carol Man, our new Girl Friday, Chief."

"Whew! Don't ever scare me like that again. Come in Carol, you might as well get used to me."

"Yes, Sir, Chief," she said, smiling at Bronski.

"Mona and Bret won't be getting married for another two weeks, so do you think our new secretary and I could take a week or two vacation?"

Frank sighed. "Oh well, if you two get married you won't be running off with her. Have a good time and be back in time for the wedding."

Carol went around the desk and kissed his cheek.

"We have to be, Chief, it's going to be a double wedding," she said with a big smile.

END

ORDER FORM

I enjoyed "Bronski" and I would like to order_____copy(s) to give to my friend(s) or family. Please find enclosed $ 12.95 + 3.95 s & h per copy ordered.

Another Lucky Bear Book I would like to order is "Bedrock Jack Philosphy" (A book on Cowboy Poetry).

Please send me_____copy(s) @ $ 3.95 each + .75 s & h per copy ordered.

Name_____

Address_____

City_____State_____Zip___

Phone#
(optional)_____

Please make checks or money orders payable to

LUCKY BEAR ENTERPRISES, INC.
P.O.Box 2506
Sparks, NV 89432-2506

Watch for "Bronski II".